What the

From Professionals:

"…he is truly a radiant human being, and I know his healing work is extraordinary." Carol Adler, President, Dandelion Books

From Workshop Participants

"Gerhard, you are a bright light and a beautiful soul." RC, workshop participant

"I really enjoyed the workshop. I came away feeling so good. I liked that it was profound and fun at the same time! I have always felt uplifted by music." VJ, workshop participant

"…thank you again for the opportunity of having had a private session with you … as well as attending last Saturday's workshop. I believe I experienced a shift and a healing in both sessions." JA, client and workshop participant

"Your gift of healing and time is still with me. I'm determined to have good days and share my joy with others, no matter what the stresses. My cells feel happy! My patience and sense of humor are back also. Happy healing!" TM

From Clients

"You bring such joy! May your blessings be returned to you manyfold." MC "(my brother) is one happy camper. He can't sit still. His toes are not stiff anymore and he can walk without any pain. His lazy eye is better. He used to see through a dark tunnel." KS

"Gerhard is amazing. I had a wonderful treatment from him today." CP

"...wanted to let you know that my 82-year-old friend with the 30-year back problem is still pain free – even his doctor can't believe it." TW

"I can't explain how it happened, but it felt like a pair of hands at work, with fingers moving in my chest. Soon my heartbeat was stabilized and the tension and pain in my chest was totally gone. I haven't had problems with my heart now for the last two years." DS

"It was a joy spending time with you...and I (am) still benefiting from the results of your healing session." JV

"He came into my life at the right time. I had just lost my partner and he made me feel better emotionally, physically, and spiritually." NN

TO: Marsha
from
Doris
Schatz

TO

Down the Ages

Journey of a Healer

**Doris Schatz
and Gerhard Kluegl**

Published by Wheatmark®
1760 East River Road, Suite 145
Tucson, Arizona 85718 U.S.A.
www.wheatmark.com

ISBN: 978-1-62787-025-2 (paperback)
ISBN: 978-1-62787-036-8 (ebook)
LCCN: 2013946116

Contents

Contents

Foreword

by Gary E. Schwartz, PhD

Imagination is more important than knowledge.
—Albert Einstein

DOWN THE AGES IS an extraordinary book about the journey and claims of Mr. Gerhard Kluegl, a remarkable energy and spiritual healer. What you are about to read will likely stretch your imagination to its limits, and then beyond. Unless you already are a firm believer in apparent miraculous healings and the existence of a greater spiritual reality, you may find yourself scratching your head from time to time, and even experiencing one or more conceptual headaches.

I am no stranger to meeting gifted psychics and energy and spiritual healers, hearing their extraordinary claims, and then attempting to test their claims in the laboratory. I have described some of this research in a number of my books including *The Afterlife Experiments* and *The Energy Healing Experiments*. I follow the scientific philosophy voiced by Carl Sagan, PhD who said "Extraordinary claims require extraordinary evidence."

I have personally witnessed amazing physical and psychological healing produced by people I call "Michael Jordans of the Healing World." I have directly observed seemingly unbelievable effects which my Western scientific Harvard education dictated must be impossible, and therefore must either be faked or caused by super-powerful placebo effects. After more than two decades of careful scientific research, I have come to the firm conclusion that not all of these extraordinary effects can be explained (away) as being the result of trickery or placebo. The truth is that some healers, and their effects, are genuine (real) and deserve our serious consideration and celebration.

However, among this group of more than forty exceptional psychics and healers, a few stand out as being especially unusual and challenging, and Mr. Gerhard Kluegl is one of them. I have done more head scratching, and experienced more conceptual headaches with him than almost anyone else. I say "almost" because I have worked with a couple of other healers who in their own ways are as paradigm challenging as Mr. Kluegl.

In chapter 15 titled "Human Energy Systems Laboratory" you will read about some of the early exploratory experiments my assistants, colleagues, and I conducted with Mr.

Kluegl (the title of my laboratory was subsequently broadened to the Laboratory for Advances in Consciousness and Health). I worked with Mr. Kluegl in various settings, not only in my laboratory, but also in my home. Based upon the totality of the evidence, I was forced to conclude that Doris Schatz's perceptions of Mr. Kluegl were more than just her imagination, and that, thanks to Doris, I had been given a special gift in coming to know Gerhard Kluegl. For the record, I do not know what percentage of Mr. Kluegl's claims and beliefs revealed in this book are actually true. If I was pressed to hazard a guess based upon my professional training as a conservative scientist, I would say "certainly less than a hundred percent." How much less? My answer would be as follows: "probably as much as my conventional western medical colleague's claims and beliefs are actually true." The reason I say this is because I have come to realize that conventional western psychology and medicine makes numerous claims and holds certain beliefs which are incomplete if not inaccurate. It seems prudent that we all keep our minds and hearts open regarding what is ultimately true concerning mechanisms of healing and health.

Importantly, as you will read in Chapter 2, Mr. Kluegl did not begin this journey as a "New Age" person. Quite the contrary, Mrs. Schatz writes that "until he was forty-two, he was a successful patent and trademark researcher." Like Albert Einstein, who also began his professional life as a patent researcher, Mr. Kluegl went far beyond his limited role in engineering applications, and they excelled beyond most people's wildest imaginations. In their own ways, it can be concluded that they became "geniuses" in their respective fields.

Mrs. Schatz has come to know Mr. Kluegl well, and she presents his (and her) journey in a clear, beautiful, and moving fashion. By the time you have completed this book, and you have pondered Mr. Kluegl's prologue about love and eternal life, followed by key inspirational quotes from Albert Schweitzer, MD, you will realize what a special gift this book is for our individual and collective lives.

Gary E. Schwartz, PhD, Professor of Psychology, Medicine, Neurology, Psychiatry, and Surgery, and Director of the Laboratory for Consciousness and Health, the University of Arizona.

1

My Story

by Doris Schatz

I've believed as many as six impossible things
before breakfast.

> —The White Queen to Alice
> in Lewis Carroll's *Alice in Wonderland*

THE WHITE QUEEN ADVISED Alice that it was easy. "You
only have to draw a long breath and shut your eyes." That
philosophy can be applied to me. However, once you begin
to believe one impossible thing, it does tend to open the
door to belief in others. At the very least, I have always
wanted to learn more about UFOs, life after death, reincarnation, life on other planets, alternate realities, and clairvoyance.

After I got to know Gerhard Kluegl, impossible things
began happening to me on a regular basis. Some of the
events required more than one long breath to believe! I
really can't write his story until I relate how I came to meet
and know him. It's an unusual story in itself.

He ranks as the most interesting person I have ever met
(and I've met some interesting people). I have to shake my

head when I think of how many turns my life had to take before I came face-to-face with Gerhard for the first time.

I am sometimes amazed by how it all happened and how many coincidences or unusual events had to happen before we came to work together. Of course, I don't believe there's any such thing as a coincidence.

I was born in Kentucky in a small town environment that should have prepared me for a clerical job at the telephone company or a teaching position. My parents were not members of any church, but my sister and I went to Sunday School and summer church camp and participated in Christian activities. I especially enjoyed gospel music. When I was about eleven, I was sent to a summer camp in Indiana where the water tasted like sulfur. There were too many prayer meetings and I was homesick. I also had a lot of questions that required better answers than I heard. In my early teens, I had read the Bible through about three times, including the genealogy chapters. I was particularly interested in the life and teachings of Jesus Christ. I never wavered from my core belief that his teachings were universal and true, even though I puzzled over some discrepancies and inconsistencies in the Bible. I attributed them to bad translations and misunderstandings of long-ago events. I understood that the Bible and its language had been manipulated by organized religion in order to retain control over the believers. My reading eventually extended to alternative religions and philosophies. I had a lot of questions that weren't answered. Most of all, I saw the hypocrisy and greed of organized religions and their thirst for power over the lives of those people who placed their souls and lives into the hands of the leaders and priests.

I read voraciously. I read history books, fairy tales, legends, myths, and historical novels. Then I discovered the occult. Hidden in a box of secondhand books purchased at an estate sale, I found an old, dusty book about spiritualism. I don't remember the title now, and the book was long ago lost, but it was the beginning of a journey. After that, I sought out those books that made me think about the true nature of things, and the feeling that I was in sight of something meaningful at all times persisted. My esoteric reading sometimes brought me a great deal of jibes and insults, like, "You don't really believe all that stuff, do you?" I did extremely well in school and was blessed with a high IQ, so it was even more astonishing to my family that I could be so gullible. But I didn't feel gullible; I felt superior. I must admit that I was sometimes arrogant that my beliefs had a better foundation than theirs. It was very satisfying for me to join Mensa, a high IQ society, and find that other so-called intelligent people were asking the same questions and reading the same books. I also found many skeptics, but these people tended to be extremely analytical and rejected anything they couldn't explain by known scientific methods.

But I also had to make a living and became a very good secretary. Using these skills, I was able to maintain several satisfying jobs during my working life, with most of my experience being as a legal secretary and then working as a paralegal for law firms in Arizona and Texas.

The year 1977 found me living in El Paso, Texas, with my husband, Don, who worked as an accountant in Juarez, Mexico, just across the international border. He introduced me to a man who was to be instrumental in writing the next chapter of my life, although I knew him only for a matter of months. He was a Frenchman, of noble birth and at least 6'5. He was married to one of my husband's accounting clerks. I'll call them Martin and Maria in this book. When I got to know him better, I learned that he was in a very unsatisfactory marriage. It seemed that he had involved himself in a scandalous affair with a student from the university where he taught. His wife of many years had divorced him. Having lost his family and high position, he married Maria, the student with whom he'd had the affair.

I was fascinated by Martin because he was an intelligent and cultivated foreigner. He told me he had attended the Sorbonne. He spoke several languages. He was a psychologist who practiced hypnosis and thought a great deal about reincarnation and the survival of the spirit. I still don't know his age, but he was older by several years than I, and he was a true citizen of the world. He had so many experiences that I never tired of our conversations. This man who I thought so wise would turn to me sometimes and say, "Can this be true? What do you think?" He had so many questions himself, and I was finally able to talk about things that I'd only read about before. Here was a man who practiced hypnosis and uncovered past lives for people. This was in 1977! A fountain of information was flowing, and I was drinking deeply. He hugged like a great bear.

His inquiring mind and questioning intellect led us to various discussions and experiments. I had been like a sponge with my reading and had never met such a well-educated man who might be interested in my opinions! He taught me hypnosis, and we experimented with past life regressions. Every session was discussed over and over while we puzzled over the implications of what we saw and experienced. We wondered if hypnosis brought forth fantasies about past lives or if those experiences being described had a basis in fact. We wondered if it was even important whether the experiences were true. We wondered if it was only important that a person's experiences under hypnosis provided a method of effecting an improvement in this life or changing negative behavior or attitudes.

We tried many things together and had some interesting results with a Ouija board. Even though I didn't believe I could be hypnotized, I agreed to an experiment. I was curious if I could recall a past life. Martin began with a countdown and suggested a very relaxed state. I enjoyed the experience, but didn't feel that I really went under. He suggested that my right arm would become numb, and I noted that it became numb, much like the numbness one felt at the dentist's office. Martin then suggested that I would be in a different body at the end of another countdown and then asked me to look at my shoes and describe them. So much for the power of suggestion, I was barefooted! And told him so! I related a story of living near Catlettburg, Tennessee, in the mountains. My husband was away and I didn't know when he'd be back. I felt he wouldn't come back. I had to work hard on the farm and take care of my little girl.

Martin moved me forward in that lifetime until I described my passing. I was thrown from a horse and hit my head on a rock at the side of the road. I was happy to leave that life and wondered what happened to the child.

Martin then brought me out of hypnosis and asked me how I felt.

"Good," I said, "but I wasn't hypnotized. I just made all that up."

He smiled. Then he said, "Look at your right hand, Doris."

I was shocked to see several large straight pins piercing my palm! There was no pain and no blood. A discussion followed (after he removed the pins) and I remembered more details of that lifetime, if that's what it was. I added that I thought my grave might still be there in a small church cemetery. We looked at the notes that Don had made and I saw that he had written Gatlinburg instead of Catlettburg. We'd been to the Smoky Mountains on a vacation trip, so he thought I was talking about that. I was positive about the spelling and corrected the notes.

We found a map of Tennessee from our vacation, but found no Catlettburg. Many years later, after I'd learned to use a computer and the internet was available for research,

I found a Catlettburg community in Sevier County, Tennessee. Someday it might be interesting to look for a grave for a woman named Louisa who was thrown from a horse.

There may be some validity to this memory. I used to enjoy horseback riding and did quite a bit, but was always very nervous when the horse was in a gallop, watching all the rocks on the right side of the horse, never on the left. I never fell off a horse in this lifetime.

My next session was more dramatic. I recalled a life in the south of France where I was burned as a heretic. Martin was there also as a revered priest with our group. I was married to the commander of a garrison and we were all past middle age. I provided a great many details and Martin made notes for this session. He was excited and intrigued because he was from the south of France and he knew a great deal about this group. I had never heard of the Cathars at that time. I thought it demonstrated some degree of psychic ability on my part and I felt that I somehow pulled this information from his mind. That in itself was impressive when you think about it!

Many years later, I ran across a book, *Holy Blood, Holy Grail*, and was excited to find that so much information in the book matched my notes, including the people, dates, and places. That book felt personal to me and I've now read it through three times.

When I discovered actual genealogical links to individuals in this group in 2012, I began to wonder about DNA and reincarnation.

Our spouses participated in some of these evenings but apparently weren't as stimulated as we were, as they soon began to flee our company and find their own amusement, ostensibly working overtime. When Martin first told me that he thought they were having an affair, I dismissed it as jealousy on his part. After all, he was French! I really thought he shouldn't be so suspicious of his wife, and I didn't believe that my husband would be capable of anything like that. I was naive. I didn't even tell Don about that conversation or Martin's suspicions. As events unfolded, however, we discovered he was right.

On June 17, 1977, we were dining with several other people at a restaurant in Juarez. It was a business dinner with business associates. Martin and I were seated next to one another, and he turned to me and said simply, "Doris, it's true... they are f———ing." Here he used an Anglo-Saxon word that didn't sound so shocking because of his charming French accent, but he said it, and I was speechless. He confided that Maria had admitted it to him earlier that evening. Someone took a snapshot right after that astonishing sentence, and I still have the photo. We both smiled for the camera, but I cannot look at that photo and not remember the sentence that preceded it and what happened later that evening.

When Don and I got home, I confronted him and asked for the truth. He admitted it and then added some hurtful details. He laughed about "doing it" in the front seat of his car! He seemed to want to unload, and he did. Everything came into the open, and I listened. I accepted all this rather quietly. There were no tears or fights that evening. We discussed it until midnight. He said that he didn't want a divorce or separation. The prospect of a divorce was frightening to me. I had no family or close friends in El Paso. What would I do?

I went to sleep that night in the guest bedroom for the first time in our ten-year marriage. At 3:00 AM, I awoke. The face of Martin was before me. I had a very strong urge to drive to Juarez and talk to him—about what, I didn't know. I just wanted to see him and talk to him. I couldn't get the thought out of my mind and felt almost that he was calling to me. I arose from bed and walked to the living room. Then I saw the clock. Of course I couldn't just drive to Mexico at this hour. What would I do? Just knock on their door? What would I say? I must be crazy. Besides, like us, he and his wife must have had their own discussion this terrible night! I decided to go back to bed, but still restless, I kept thinking of him. His face wouldn't leave me. I arose again and went to the phone with the idea to call him. Again, a crazy idea, but it wouldn't go away. I was very distressed, but common sense prevailed, and I finally went back to bed and fell into an unusually deep sleep without making that call.

At six thirty the next morning, Don came to the bedroom door and woke me up. He told me that he was going to pick up Maria and then go to the office to work on the inventory. Still half asleep, I sat straight up and exclaimed, "Don't go—one or both of them are dead!" I was as shocked by this statement as he was. He looked at me and told me that I was crazy and left the room. I was a bit astonished and distressed at this outburst myself. Amazingly enough, I fell back into a sound sleep after he left.

I awoke naturally around 8:30 AM and went to the dining room for breakfast. The earlier events of the day, including my premonition, had been pushed to the back of my mind. I don't recall now what was in my heart and mind. Maybe I thought everything would sort itself out somehow. I heard the garage door open and Don walked into the dining room, ashen faced. He looked at me and stated simply, "Martin is dead." I was stunned and remembered my earlier outburst. I don't remember whatever we said to one another after that, but I wanted to blame him, to strike out. At the same time, I was also thinking that it was my fault, that I should have gone to him the night before.

I was shaking and asked Don to drive me to Juarez—I had to see Martin. I had to see if it was true that he was dead. I must have felt I could change something. When we arrived, I saw two or three police officers in the living room with Maria. I just looked at Maria without speaking. The officers allowed me into Martin's office.

When I saw him lying on the floor, I knew that his spirit was no longer there. I touched his hand and said good-bye. Don told me that Martin had turned on the gas to a little space heater and died of asphyxiation. Somehow I didn't accept it. It didn't feel true.

The next few days were a blur of horrible emotions. I placed all the blame for his death on Don and Maria. For a number of reasons and because of many mysterious occurrences after this event, I didn't and couldn't accept that it was suicide. I spent the next twenty-three years of my life believing that Martin was murdered. The psychic contact that I believe was made between Martin and me at the time of his death was an important event in my lifelong pursuit of proof of survival of the spirit after death. I believe that my friend came to me in the hour of his passing and that a strong psychic bond survives to this day with that gentle bear who was not my father, husband, brother, or lover, but nevertheless a companion soul.

After this horrible night, my life changed drastically. There was no turning back. My marriage was in shambles. My husband, previously a nonsmoker, began chain-smoking on the patio and thinking about his role in this sordid mess. He felt haunted by the ghost of Martin to the point that he heard Martin's voice when he was driving to work. He once left the house for work and returned home within fifteen minutes. He was clearly in some sort of shock. He went to the patio and sat down, trembling. I was sure there'd been an auto accident and asked what had happened.

He told me that Martin was talking to him. He could hear his voice in the car. Don didn't believe in such things and didn't understand what was happening. This was clearly more than he could handle. His guilty conscience and hearing Martin's voice brought him to a point where he couldn't function. He finally packed his bag and left.

A few months later he filed for and obtained an uncontested divorce.

It was about this time that I traveled to Scottsdale, Arizona, and took part in a seminar with Dick Sutphen, a past life regression hypnotist, and learned more about this subject.

For a long time, I was an unhappy divorcée and felt I had no chance for any more relationships with men. I had lots of free time for my esoteric pursuits, though, and these I indulged, reading and reading and reading. I would float in and out of psychic development groups but never focused on any one topic for deeper study. I kept my interest in hypnosis and past life regressions because of some memories and personal experiences regarding a past life in France, which I felt I had shared with Martin. In this past life, we were both burned as heretics. Other past life memories surfaced over the years, but the dominant one was in the south of France. Wherever I went, I looked for evidence of that reality in my life. And I found it often.

I have believed in reincarnation since the first moment I heard about it. It felt true and logical then, and I have found the proof of it in my life over and over again. I often wondered why Martin didn't contact me through any one of the psychics and mediums and astrologers I met in my travels, but I never got one solid indication from him in the twenty-three years that followed his death. That and that alone sometimes made me question my belief in survival of the spirit. I thought that if anyone could come through, it would be him, especially after that night visitation when he died.

When I met my future husband, Franz, I was tired of the single life. Here was another foreigner—a German this time, tall and blond with blue eyes and a courtly bearing.

He came with two sons, Michael and Robert, aged twelve and ten. I fell in love with all of them, quit my job with only a few misgivings, and crossed the ocean to become a wife and mother at the age of forty-seven! I learned a new culture, a new language, and a new role. Sometimes, I didn't do so well at anything and wanted to return to America. The rewards came with time. Franz and the boys that we raised to young men are the greatest blessings in my life today.

We were living in Landshut, a beautiful medieval town in Bavaria. I was learning to speak the language and had found my place in their society. I didn't remain a hausfrau (housewife) for very long. I joined a professional country-rock band where I sang and played guitar. We played music many weekends and often traveled around Europe in our band bus. This experience was very valuable because I learned to stand in front of a group and talk and sing and play music. It was also a lot of fun! I tired of the schedule after a few years and found work near home as an English teacher for adults. I taught at BMW and other businesses as well as at the community college. I found that I liked teaching.

During this time, my esoteric pursuits were totally confined to reading. I found no groups who shared my interest in the community where I lived. Our friends were Franz's family and associates. We made other friends at the bridge table. I had some music friends. I only had one close friend, a British lady, with whom I could discuss my beliefs. She was the one who told me about the healer.

A bridge friend of ours was ill with terminal cancer, and we were all very concerned for him. We arranged for his picture to be sent to the healer, who agreed to try absent healing. The cancer was very advanced, and the healing didn't take place as hoped.

Just as we were getting ready to leave Germany and

return to the United States to live, we were invited to an Easter celebration. Our friends owned a 360-year-old farmhouse in Bavaria. I always enjoyed visiting them. Although my husband was out of the country on a bridge trip, I accepted. I always had such fun with these people, and they had interesting friends.

Among the guests was a lovely elderly couple who lived nearby. I loved them both immediately. I found that I shared an interest in genealogy with the lady and that we possibly shared a common ancestor. That ancestor was from the south of France and possibly connected with the same group I had described in my past life regression hypnosis experiment.

Her husband, Josef, however, had just recovered from a serious illness that had required hospitalization and baffled the doctors. In fact, they had almost given up on finding a successful treatment for him. He had suffered from a digestive difficulty and was thought to be dying. He was barely able to eat enough to live and had lost a great deal of weight. He even had to be fed intravenously during this time. Now there he was, at our Easter party, fit and active, and eating everything on his plate! He was also happily playing with a set of dowsing rods that he had newly acquired and was the life of the party!

Josef was eager to tell us how his cure had taken place. The healer had, just by feeling his aura, explained that in a previous lifetime, he was killed in a surprise attack by someone he considered a friend. The friend suddenly and inexplicably stabbed him in the throat with a knife. His aura had been imprinted with this knife and wound, which had surfaced again in his current life. He was suddenly unable to swallow any food or drink.

When the doctors were unable to locate the problem, they turned to a healer. The healer "found" the injury in the aura and then treated it with surgical instruments.

12

He also said it was important to understand the origin of the problem as being from a past life. It was important to love and forgive the friend who had attacked him without warning. Only then was it possible for the healing to take place.

Josef explained that his illness had occurred at the exact age he had been when the attack happened in the previous life. It was as if the subconscious "recalled" the attack and re-experienced the effect. A repressed memory had been released. This happened in March 1999. Josef survived another ten years with no recurrence of the problem, eventually dying of an unrelated illness at the age of eighty-six.

Meeting the Healer

I was determined to meet this healer. I had some questions. Why did this problem wait until Josef was an old man? If it had happened in a previous life, why hadn't he been born with the problem? How had the healing taken place? I had never been particularly interested in healers, but on the other hand, I'd never seen a healer up close. Here was my chance. I always thought that miraculous healings took place because of the belief system of the person to be healed and by some kind of autosuggestion or hypnosis. I believe in reincarnation and karma, so it wasn't a stretch for me to accept the supposed reason for the illness. I was more than a little curious. I asked how I could get an appointment.

Two months later, my husband, a friend, and I found ourselves in his waiting room. I brought my husband as someone who needed a healing. He had a lot of back and shoulder pain, which the doctors hadn't been able to heal. I must tell you that my husband doesn't believe in these things. He thinks we're a little cuckoo. That's a form of harmless insanity! However, we wanted to watch how the healer worked, and he agreed to accompany us.

We drove to a very nice house in a newer neighborhood and met a soft-spoken and modest middle-aged man named Gerhard Kluegl, who looked as if he could be a clerk or postal supervisor. Was it my imagination that his blue eyes pierced right through me as he took my hand? He was neatly and conservatively dressed, and his home was tasteful and simply furnished.. There was a candle and a bit of incense. Books on the coffee table indicated that we shared some reading interests. We observed German custom and formally addressed him as Herr Kluegl.

I really didn't know what to expect, so I just watched him. I had no prior personal experience with a healer. I think I expected more drama. He didn't do any laying on of hands. He didn't shout, "Be healed!" and push the sufferer in the middle of the forehead as I'd seen on television, with helpers catching the people as they fell to the floor. He didn't do any blood and guts psychic surgery like the Philippine healers I saw on television. So, to me, he was different.

I took a seat on the sofa, and Herr Kluegl began the healing session by asking Franz if he had permission to feel his aura. Franz agreed, and the healer raised his arms over his head and brought them slowly down and around Franz's body in a pyramidal pattern. He would occasionally pause, make small motions with his hands, and then ask a question. How does this feel? Can you feel this? Franz's replies all seemed to be in the negative. One would have thought he had no problems at all.

As I watched him, I sensed the utmost sincerity and honesty. There were no pious platitudes, no religious exhortations, no dramatics. Here was an intelligent, well-spoken man who seemed to honestly care about the person before him and how that person felt.

When the healing session was over, we walked out to our car. The healer followed us, and as I turned to shake his hand, I impulsively called him Gerhard instead of Herr

Kluegl and hugged him! He looked momentarily startled, then obviously remembered that I'm an American. He pardoned my breach of etiquette and smiled back at me warmly. I even invited this stranger to visit us in Arizona. We were preparing for our move back to America at that time. I gave him our card with the Arizona address and phone number.

There's no explanation for why I departed from formal German custom at that moment and invited a virtual stranger to visit us. I now believe it was prompted by my higher self. It certainly wasn't anything to which I had given any thought before that moment! It might have been the gentle stirring of a past life memory. Thus began a close friendship, which continues to this day.

Franz would not have been rated as one of Gerhard's most successful healings at that time. Of course, he wasn't very open to this type of healing then and went with us out of curiosity. It was not a dramatic healing. No past lives were explained; my husband wouldn't have accepted them if they had been. Somehow, his headaches became less severe, and his back pain diminished to the point that he hardly complains now in spite of a very active lifestyle, including hiking in the mountains, playing table tennis, and swimming. Shortly after that healing appointment, we packed our bags and moved back to Arizona. Gerhard was placed in the back of my mind as an interesting experience—until he faxed us in America that he would like to come and visit us for seven days! I had invited him to come, after all. Germans don't do that lightly. Not only was he coming to visit us in Arizona, he said that he'd like to do healing while he was here. I have to admit that I was more than a bit distressed by my impulsive invitation and his acceptance. What was I to do with him? I didn't know where to start.

There I was, just returned to the area after a long

absence and looking for people who needed a healing! Oh, but I had an entire month to find some contacts. I did the only thing I could think of: I opened the yellow pages and called some local spiritualist churches. Fortunately for me, they were perfectly open to host him and even extended invitations to speak to their members and perhaps give a demonstration. I was happy, and Gerhard was happy.

After Gerhard's first visit to America, Franz began to suspect that something out of the ordinary was occurring in his living room. He personally witnessed many happy clients and a few healings and improvements that were so dramatic that people in the room were reduced to tears. He now recommends Gerhard to anyone who is suffering but still believes it's not for him.

I never expected that I would be associated with a spiritual healer, but it happened. I've had some confounding experiences with Gerhard. Nothing ever really surprises him anymore because so many unusual things have happened. Recently, I stumbled across a web page that was established for the sole purpose of debunking him and anyone foolish enough to follow him. At first, I was insulted for him, myself, and the thousands of people who have come to him for help. Then I realized that this was a natural result of his newfound stature and success!

I've discovered that I too have psychic gifts and have come to believe that we all have them in varying degrees. I now have a better understanding of the psychic and mediumship experiences that I've had my entire life. I'm not surprised when I meet earthbound entities or feel a presence. When I'm working late at night, sometimes my hair is stroked and my shoulder gets patted. I know then that it's time for rest and someone is watching out for me.

I've felt earthbound entities, loved them, and released them. I've seen people cry with joy because they're free of pain after years of not being helped by conventional doctors.

I've had telephone calls speaking of miraculous recoveries and surgeries being cancelled by doctors when they couldn't find the tumor that was on the X-rays the week before. I've had people tell me that Gerhard is a master, and I believe them. I know that I am blessed to call him a friend.

2

Who Is Gerhard Kluegl?

True knowledge is when one knows the limitations of one's knowledge.

—Lao-Tse

GERHARD IS A HEALER, but he was not born one. Until he was forty-two, he was a successful patent and trademark researcher with his own business. Then, he became a full-time practicing aura surgeon. Since that time, he has seen and helped thousands of people; participated in numerous research projects with scientists, institutes, and universities; conducted workshops and seminars all over the world; and been the subject of several documentaries and film projects, and made several television appearances.

He is not a traditional surgeon with university training, although he uses a wide array of knives, scalpels, needles, syringes, and scissors in his work. He operates just a few centimeters away from the skin, moving his hands and instruments in the energy field, called the human aura. Many of his healings are subtle, but some can only be classified as miracles. To Gerhard, there are no miracles—just a healing that has taken place that modern medicine, as we understand it today, cannot explain.

This book is about how he discovered his innate abilities and developed them into a greater understanding of the universe and our place therein.

Gerhard sometimes gives the impression that he comes from another world. In some respects, he does. When I first met him, he lived in Landshut, a beautiful medieval town in southeastern Germany. Landshut was a glamorous capital city in the Middle Ages. It would be the capital city and heart of Bavaria today if a childless marriage hadn't handed the ruling authority to another branch of the family. Munich won that right but paid dearly in the bombing of World War II. Landshut was mostly spared, with the only real damage suffered at the railway station. The castle, churches, and residences today remain one of the best-kept scenic secrets of Lower Bavaria. It's easy to imagine it as it appeared in 1571 because it hasn't changed that much. The streets in the old part of Landshut are wide avenues of cobblestone. Burg Trausnitz, a medieval castle with a moat now filled with rose bushes, towers over these cobblestone boulevards in the old part of town. The architecture is a mixture of Romanesque, Gothic, and Renaissance, and the result is beautiful.

Gerhard's parents were refugees from wartorn Czechoslovakia in the aftermath of World War II. Born in Treuchtlingen, Germany, the oldest of two sons, Gerhard grew up in a traditional Catholic home. His father worked for the German Railway, and his mother was a housewife.

Gerhard had a very normal childhood in postwar Germany. At an early age, he was very devout and so spiritually inclined that he, his family, and friends always assumed that he would enter the priesthood. At the last moment, for reasons he still doesn't understand, he abruptly changed his mind and stepped back from enrollment in the seminary. He now feels that the priesthood was not a part of his life plan.

After he finished his formal schooling, Gerhard began his professional life. He followed his father into the German Railway System, where he worked for three years. Then, in 1967, he became an apprentice in the German patent office in Munich. Gerhard toiled in the bowels of this gargantuan building as he learned the tools of his trade. He examined design and trademark applications to determine if they were complete and accurate and that the correct filing fees had been paid. While completing these mundane tasks, he found it necessary to visit the library of the German Patent Office quite often. There, he could bury himself in the massive books and read about scientific innovations and discoveries. He was particularly interested in air travel and pored over aerospace journals. He studied aircraft designs whenever he had the opportunity.

He read indexes, studied applications, and sat in front of large books for hours on end. He collected a good deal of information on scientific subjects and mechanical engineering—good, solid descriptions of workable inventions with blueprints. There was nothing ethereal or spiritual there— just nuts, bolts, and diagrams.

In 1972, he decided to resign from the German Patent Office to become an independent patent and trademark researcher.

With his gentle humor, he does not miss the fact that his chosen profession required sketches, working models, blueprints, and diagrams. There is no working model for becoming a healer, however, and the paths to spiritual understanding are many. Each person must find his or her own way, and one is lucky to find a mentor or spiritual advisor. Gerhard believes that he was guided by a higher source, until he could do nothing else but be a healer.

Gradually, he devoted more and more of his private

time and energy to spiritual healing until it became his full-time pursuit. He has traveled to England, Finland, Austria, Holland, Scotland, Spain, Italy, Denmark, Switzerland, the Philippines, the Netherlands, the Ukraine, and the United States, where he has held private and public healing demonstrations, workshops, and experiments. His first trip to America was in March 2000 when I invited him to Tucson, Arizona. He stayed a short seven days. In that brief period, he spoke to several groups and saw many individuals privately, and the reaction was overwhelming!

He's not the seventh son of a seventh son, and he wasn't born with any obvious special talents. In the course of following his hobby, he discovered an unusually good aptitude for dowsing. Dowsing is traditionally associated with searching for water or mineral deposits with a rod or willow branch, but modern-day dowsers will use these methods to discover answers to questions, locate missing objects, find water, and so on. He has never considered himself to be a psychic or medium. He recalls nothing from his childhood to point in this direction. He says he often felt different from the other children. This in itself is certainly not unusual. Gerhard only discovered this gift of healing when he was over forty. He remarked recently that he himself is frequently more astonished by some of the occurrences in his workshops and healing sessions than the persons in attendance.

In England, a second home to Gerhard, he feels most comfortable with the people, their customs, and their language. He visits as often as he can, and he is particularly knowledgeable about the spiritualists who abound there. He believes the British mediums and spiritualists are of the highest quality. Whereas many mediums speak in generalities and platitudes, the down-to-earth Brits are full of facts. They can be quite specific when giving predictions and indeed don't make predictions or give messages unless they are specific.

In April 1989, during one of his frequent visits to London, he made it a point to consult with several famous mediums. Each told him separately that he had healing energy in his hands. Some spiritual doctors, speaking through mediums, told him they were ready to help him in this pursuit if he wished to do healing. With so many indications of this latent gift, Gerhard began some private experimentation and research and, to his own astonishment, discovered that it was true. He believes that he is being helped by beings who were physicians in their earthly lifetimes and knows several by name. Upon research, he has been able to verify the existence of several of these doctors. One of his doctors is a Russian woman who is an expert on gynecological issues.

I once asked Gerhard if he had ever had doubts about what he was doing. He said he never took a healing for granted and was full of wonder each time a healing appeared to take place. When asked if he is able to heal someone or something, his response is always, "I will try."

He eventually moved to the Principality of Liechtenstein, where he lives in a beautiful Alpine village. He is occupied full time with healing activities. He often travels to the offices of naturopaths and alternative medicine practitioners in Switzerland, Austria, and Germany. He particularly enjoys working with doctors and health care professionals. He conducts healing workshops in other countries and travels at every opportunity and invitation to present his healing to a growing audience. He is most eager to show people that they can be their own healers. He believes that anyone can learn to feel this energy of the universe and help himself or herself and others with this knowledge. He claims to derive the most energy from helping others.

One thing is very clear about this healing energy he uses: it's not his energy.

He can work for hours without stopping, and he doesn't

seem to get tired at all. He only reluctantly pauses for a glass of water or piece of fruit or to take a bathroom break, but he hurries back to his waiting subjects. He can work with people all day and feel only slightly fatigued because he stands so long. His personal energy does not appear to be depleted. On the contrary, he is exhilarated and energetic at the end of a healing day. He feels as if a special, powerful light illumines each and every cell of his body.

He believes that the energy is something he can pull from the universe and that he is only a conduit, much like an electric cord plugged in the wall outlet. He also believes that alcohol will depress or block this energy, so he doesn't indulge if a healing is on the calendar in the next twenty-four hours. Even when he has no healings planned, he will only have one glass of wine or a light beer with his meal, believing that alcohol will inhibit divine energy from manifesting in the highest and best way.

Some movie and television producers have become interested in energy healing and attempted to bring this to the public as entertainment and information. Gerhard has made many television appearances and would like to bring the information on healing to a larger number of people, but the very nature of healing is intensely personal and doesn't seem to lend itself to a 10-minute demonstration on a talk show.

Career Highlights

In April 2005, Gerhard was the first spiritual healer to be awarded the Alternative European Medicine Prize, established by Dr. Ingeborg Gebert-Heiss, at a healer forum at the Bodensee (Lake Constance) in Radolfzell, Germany.

In 2006, *Der Mensch, ein Geistiges Wesen (Man, a Spiritual Being)* was filmed under the auspices of SHP Akademie, Fuchstal, Germany. SHP Akademie is an academy formed by Clemens Kuby, a documentary film maker, to explore the nature of self healing processes. Mr. Kuby was seriously injured in a fall when he was a young man. He was told he would be a quadraplegic for the rest of his life, but refused to accept the diagnosis. He believes he healed himself by thinking himself well. When he asked his doctors how the healing came about, the only response was that it was spontaneous. They didn't know how or why. To Kuby, that wasn't satisfactory, and he set out to discover how this self-healing worked. The documentary, a collection of lectures by Clemens Kuby about spiritual healing, featured Gerhard as a healer with unusual abilities. Gerhard and Mr. Kuby share an intense curiousity about the mechanics of this phenomena.

In autumn 2007, Dr. Michael Ehrenberger, an Austrian physician who owns and operates TV-Gesundheit, a health and wellness television network, interviewed Gerhard. Gerhard described his healing methods and demonstrated with anatomical models how he performed aura surgery. The segment, "Interview With An Aura Surgeon," aired on January 15, 2008. At the time of this printing, the interview is still available online at http://marktplatz-gesundheit.at/blog/aura-chirurgie.

In April 2010, Beate Lehner produced a feature film, *Ich Sehe was, was du nicht siehst—Von Heilern, Wunderheilern, und der Suche nach dem Glück* (I See Something You Don't See—About Healers, Miracle Workers, and the Search for Happiness). SWR 2, a German television network, broadcast the film.

In June 2010, Giselle Camenisch produced *Ich bin ein Weltenmensch— Heilen in der Aura* (I Am a Universal Man—Healing in the Aura), an attempt to document the undiscovered potential of human beings. Gerhard demonstrates and explains his aura surgery techniques in this documentary. The film shows him working in cooperation with doctors of medicine and specialists. The film documents cases where his aura surgery has had demonstrable results in the physical body, some of which might be termed miraculous.

The documentary aired on 3SAT, a public, commercial-free television network in Germany, Austria, and Switzerland. It declared itself to be a journey into the world of spirit, where life has neither a beginning nor an end. The film succeeded in unleashing a flood of public interest, including the usual scorn and ridicule. An avalanche of e-mail and telephone calls followed, and Gerhard was deluged with requests for appointments.

The producer observed and filmed Gerhard as he performed his aura surgery. At that time, Gerhard estimated that he had performed over ten thousand of these procedures. The film documented Gerhard as he worked, using actual surgical instruments to straighten spines, treat wounds, and even align teeth..

The documentary included interviews with doctors and patients who were very positive about their experiences with Gerhard. Hopefully, this book will introduce Gerhard to an American audience, help bring the subject of energy healing to light, and provide assistance for those who need understanding and healing in their lives.

In March 2012, Arkana Verlag, a Random House publisher in Germany, published *Quantenland—Ein Leben als Aurachirurg,* (*Quantumland - The Life of an Aura Surgeon*) coauthored by Gerhard and Tom Fritze. The authors explore the phenomenon of aura surgery and the connection with what we know as quantum physics and the so-called miracles of energy healing. The book documents many of Gerhard's successful healings and places them within a new and exciting context.

For the first time, Gerhard's method of healing and his successes with the morphogenetic fields described by

Rupert Sheldrake can be documented. The book attempts to explain Werner Heisenberg's Uncertainty Principle in a plausible manner. It is currently in its third printing, and a Russian translation is planned. *Quantenland* is the first time that we can connect quantum physics and the long-observed miracle cures achieved by aura surgeons. As a side note, Clemens Kuby is Werner Heisenberg's nephew.

Along with his associate, Dr. Folker Meissner, Gerhard has founded the International Academy of Aura Surgery for advanced training in this new and exciting field that is grounded in quantum physics. A workshop is already planned for early 2014 in Hong Kong.

Gerhard himself is a modest, unassuming gentleman with a kindly smile. His healing methods produce no dramatic manifestations, just healing. Pain and disease disappear. Surgically removed ovaries grow back and tonsils are removed without conventional surgery.

This book is not written for scientists who are concerned with morphogenetic fields or uncertainty principles. It's simply about a healer who goes about his daily business of making people better and exploring his own gifts.

3

The Healer's Education

The most beautiful and most profound experience is the sensation of the mystical. It is the sower of all true science. He to whom this emotion is a stranger, who can no longer wonder and stand rapt in awe, is as good as dead. To know that what is impenetrable to us really exists, manifesting itself as the highest wisdom and the most radiant beauty which our dull faculties can comprehend only in their primitive forms—this knowledge, this feeling is at the center of true religiousness.

—Albert Einstein, The Merging of Spirit and Science

GERHARD MARRIED, AND HE and his wife traveled to Italy for a holiday in April 1983. As he reports it, "I brought a book with me about saving money and reducing taxes. At the end of that book, there was a tip that I could lessen my tax burden by learning a new occupation, and there was a notice about building biology. I thought that building biologist would be a nice title to have. When I came home, I wrote to an institute near Rosenheim and got information about the course. At the same time, we decided to build a house of our own."

Building Biology

It was income taxation that really got Gerhard interested in building biology; it was building biology that got him interested in geobiology; it was geobiology that got him interested in dowsing; and it was dowsing that brought him to healing.

Before that time, he didn't know anything about earth rays or radiation, but that topic was listed in the course information. He wasn't sure he even believed in earth rays! His curiosity was aroused enough to make some inquiries, and he got an address for a dowser. He invited the dowser to visit their new home near Landshut. When the dowser arrived, he started at the outside of the house and walked around with his dowsing rods. He came inside and made notes on a floor plan. He then used that floor plan to plot the earth's radiation lines. He told them their bed was located in the worst possible place in the house. Gerhard wondered if that was why his feet and legs were always cold. He was in the habit of wearing socks to bed, which prompted many jokes and remarks from his wife. He wore the socks even in summer! He suffered with many colds, and his resistance seemed to be weak. At the suggestion of the dowser, the bed was moved to the other side of the room. After that, he no longer needed the socks in bed. Surprisingly, his health also seemed to be a lot better.

Geobiology, Georadiation, and Dowsing

This experience, of course, aroused his curiosity, and he wanted to learn more about dowsing. He investigated further and discovered that a geobiology class was being taught in Schwabing, which is in the northern part of Munich. The address was familiar; he discovered that the course was being taught directly behind the German Patent Office where he had worked twelve years ago. His new interest had brought him back to this familiar place.

The instructor for the geobiology course was a medical doctor who was also a geologist and had an additional degree in forestry! It was there that Gerhard learned about the earth's energy and radiation. Everything was new and exciting, and he proved to be an eager and apt student—even a gifted one. The dowsing rods came alive in his hands, and he felt connected to the Earth. He was astonished that such an energy field could exist and that he had never heard of it before. More astonishing, very few other people even seemed to be consciously aware of it or display any interest in it! He discovered that he could locate water and find out how deep it was located in the ground. He discovered that he was a good dowser and could get answers to questions that he would pose in his mind.

Dowsing is considered to be a method of reaching the superconscious mind. The question must be carefully phrased and able to be answered with a simple yes or no. For example, the question could be, "Is there potable water to be found in this location?" If the answer is yes, then the next question might be, "Can this water be located 100-200 feet deep?" and so on. It is important for the dowser to hold the question in his or her mind and not to lose focus.

A dowser may use a willow branch, metal rods, a pendulum, or just his body to determine where energy flows and if the energy is beneficial or harmful to humans. Gerhard learned that what is good for certain animals is not necessarily good for others.

The willow branch, metal rods, or pendulum will respond in the dowser's hands by pulling down or out or to the side. A dowser must practice and learn his technique to determine how the equipment responds to his energy. Of course, the learning phase must take place with questions where the answer is known in advance. "Is my name John?" might be a learning question for the instrument.

Gerhard learned about manmade radiation emanating from power lines and transformers. He learned which building materials were healthy and which were not so healthy to use in construction of a house. He learned how to bring harmony into a house. He learned about earth's radiation, magnetic currents, solar rays, and the effects of running water deep under the earth's surface. He learned about the grid patterns circling the Earth. He found and studied ley lines, Hartmann Grids, Curry lines, and geomagnetic energies. For Gerhard, studying building biology was like reading a well-written novel. He simply couldn't stop learning about it—it was that exciting!

One day, an instructor drove up from Salzburg to teach the class the techniques for using a pendulum. At the end of the instruction period, she drew a circle on the board and explained to the students that the circle represented the city of Salzburg. Outside the circle, she drew seven smaller circles and wrote names on them. She said that these smaller circles represented the suburbs of Salzburg. She showed them how to hold their left hands aloft as a kind of antenna and try to find the energy from her aura. Then, holding a pendulum in the right hand, the students were to ask the pendulum to find the suburb in which she lived. There were forty people in the class, but only five were able to discover the right suburb. Gerhard was one of the five.

A year and a half later, he took his examination. When he turned in his voluminous research paper, the professor remarked dryly that he hadn't expected a doctoral work. Gerhard had found it very natural and simple to bring all that he had learned to the examination. He just kept writing and writing and writing. He couldn't stop sharing this new knowledge with others, either. He had found something exciting to do.

At this time, he lived in a small village near Landshut. In the village, there was an old castle, which went back to the time of Roman occupation. He had always been fascinated by this castle and often wished he could find a reason to visit it to see it up close. It was a privately owned castle and was therefore not open to the public. He heard that it was owned by a baroness and that she was a very reclusive individual who avoided contact with her neighbors.

When he finished his studies in geobiology, he received several invitations to speak on the subject. He was happy to share what he had learned with others. One of those invitations was from the local garden society.

As a result of this presentation, he received a telephone call from the baroness. She asked him if he would be interested in visiting her to examine the chapel. The chapel was a separate structure from the old castle, but Gerhard was delighted at this opportunity and eagerly accepted.

When he arrived at the castle, he found the baroness to be very cordial and extraordinarily interested in what he had to tell her about earth radiation and dowsing. He was totally astonished that she already possessed a great deal of knowledge about this subject, which was still so new to him. After their initial conversation, she and Gerhard went to the chapel, and he proceeded to use his dowsing rods to discover what he could.

As he circled the chapel with his dowsing rods, he saw a pedestal in the chapel. This pedestal possessed a powerful energy, which was unique to his experience. This pedestal was located directly in front of the altar. As he moved outside the chapel, he found a spot on the ground just outside the chapel that seemed to have an identical energy to the pedestal. It is extremely rare for two different spots to radiate the same energy, and Gerhard remarked on this to the baroness. He told her that he believed that the Romans had placed a sacrificial altar or pedestal at these places, where offerings might be made to the gods and goddesses. The baroness then used the side of her foot to clear a place in the gravel, and they discovered the foundation of an old Roman pedestal directly on the spot where Gerhard had located the powerful energy. The pedestal itself had been removed or lost long ago, but its energy was still evident and powerful.

Gerhard and the baroness then re-entered the chapel to take another look at the pedestal before the altar. The pedestal in the chapel had been placed there many centuries ago. Gerhard could see that the pedestal was being used as a work bench and that the surface had been damaged. Gerhard received a strong feeling that it was wrong to use this consecrated spot for cutting and chipping and hammering; and the spiritual energy here had been profaned by this activity.

The baroness then related a story to him. "For many years," she told Gerhard, "blackbirds have been coming to the west wing of the castle [directly facing the chapel], and they beat with their wings against the windows until they collapse and fall on the ground in exhaustion. Then, when they recovered, they would just fly away." She went on to tell him that this happened every day at exactly six o'clock in the morning. This was so disturbing and frightening to the cleaning woman that she refused to enter any rooms in the west wing for cleaning. The baroness wondered if there was a connection with the disturbed energy and the birds' behavior.

Gerhard believed that the chapel—in particular, the pedestal located before the altar—needed a healing, but he didn't know exactly how to proceed. Suddenly, he remembered he had a friend who had studied Kahuna magic, which is a Hawaiian form of healing and energy. He thought his friend could work alongside him, and he proposed the idea to the baroness. She agreed that his friend could come with him to try a healing ceremony in and around the chapel.

Some days later, the friend arrived, and they entered the chapel and held a short healing meditation. The baroness remained outside the chapel and left them to their business. After they finished their meditation and came out of the chapel, the baroness told them that she had felt a change in the air. During the meditation itself, there was absolutely no air movement, and she felt that the air became very still and smooth, as if something had been calmed.

Gerhard's friend happened to be very sensitive and was a medium. He explained to them that he could feel some earthbound souls around the castle. Gerhard understood about earthbound souls but had no idea about how to release them at that time. He resolved to learn more about these earthbound entities.

Two days later, he received a call from the baroness, who told him that the blackbirds had not come to the west wing windows the next morning. Indeed, since that time, they have never returned to the castle.

He didn't forget about the earthbound entities at the castle that his friend had mentioned. Gerhard studied the subject, and six months later, he finally felt that he had enough information about releasing earthbound souls and was eager to put his knowledge to use. It was an extremely cold and bitter day in January when he returned to the castle alone. He wanted to try to release the souls and complete the healing of the chapel. The baroness opened the gate. Her large, black dog began barking wildly from the castle, where he was confined in a room. The dog had never barked before when Gerhard arrived, but this time, he would not be quiet. The baroness left Gerhard in the courtyard and retreated to her castle to quiet the dog.

He had planned it thoroughly. He had brought dowsing rods, a pendulum, a simple compass, tape recorder with loudspeaker, some music tapes, four small candles, and some incense. He planned to create a light cross in the four directions with the candles. He held the compass in his hand, but the needle didn't move! He shook the compass, thinking the needle had gotten stuck somehow in transit. It still didn't work, so he set it aside.

Then, he set the tape player down and put in a music cassette. The tape player seemed to have no power. He had installed brand-new batteries in it at home before leaving, and it had worked perfectly. What was going on here? It was frustrating, but Gerhard knew that he must continue. He used the pendulum to locate the four cardinal directions and placed the candles on the ground and lit them. At the exact moment the fourth candle was lit, the tape player started playing Mozart's Requiem. Gerhard then felt a hot energy appear in the palms of both hands, and he knew he was ready to begin.

He asked for any and all earthbound souls to use the music to leave the place and the building. He was standing under a balcony of the castle with his arms outstretched and his hands open. In spite of the cold, he could feel his hands glowing with the heat that had come into them. At the same time, he could feel a bitter, cold energy that rushed past his legs, whipping his pants legs around him violently. He was not afraid. On the contrary, he felt a beautiful and peaceful energy that had enveloped his entire body. Suddenly, the wind stopped, and there was a still, mild feeling all around him.

He knew that his work had been done. He had no idea

how many souls had been trapped in the area, but knew that they were no longer present and everything was calm. He also knew that a new and important chapter had begun in his life.

He went to retrieve his tools. The compass was now working perfectly. He passed by a window of the castle and glanced in. The dog was curled up peacefully on the floor and apparently sleeping.

One week later, there was a strong hurricane in Bavaria. The baroness telephoned to tell him that she saw the tall, old pine trees bowing to the ground in the wild and fierce winds. She was very afraid that a falling tree might destroy the roof of the castle. Hurricanes are highly unusual in Bavaria, and the storm had knocked down entire forests of tall pine trees. Even though many pine trees surrounding her property were laid flat by the hurricane, not a single tree on her property and within her fence was destroyed! Since that time, Gerhard and the baroness have become very close friends, and he has received many invitations to visit her in her fine old castle.

House Dowsing

Gerhard began to do house examinations on a regular basis.

Since his mother had died of breast cancer in October 1983, he had many reasons to think about her suffering and their relationship. He had learned about geopathic zones and that cancer could occur if a bed or workspace were placed in an area with harmful energy. Europe has been the leader in research on geopathic stress zones. Gerhard wanted to help people create safe, healthy spaces for living, working, and sleeping.

In brief, for our readers, Hartmann Grids are lines that run north-south and east-west, creating a checkerboard of electromagnetic earth currents. The Curry Net runs diagonal to the Hartmann Grid, running northwest to southeast and southwest to northeast. Dowsers state that when all of these lines and water intersect, a zone will be created where plant life, animal life, and human life can be affected negatively.

One of the first house examinations he conducted was in Moosburg. A man was suffering from a malignant brain tumor and was experiencing horrible pain. Gerhard visited the house, found the outside points of the radiation, and brought those points into the floor plan. He found a crossing point and located the bed in this floor plan. He discovered that there was a very negative energy directly under the patient's bed. He instructed the family to move the bed to the other side of the room. Some months later, he heard from a mutual acquaintance that the man had died, but his suffering had been greatly relieved just by relocating the bed.

In another case, he was contacted by a woman about her husband, who was suffering from cancer of the jawbone. When Gerhard arrived, he noticed a very strange and unpleasant smell in the house. The doctor had given the poor man only three or four weeks to live, and he was in terrible pain. By dowsing, Gerhard discovered that the bed was in the worst possible location, with crossing of underground water, Hartmann Grids, and Curry lines. He advised them to move the bed, which they did. Unfortunately, it was too late for the patient, but the family and medical practitioners noticed that the unpleasant smell dissipated and the patient's pain was somewhat relieved.

In his reading and workshops, Gerhard had learned that organ music by Bach brings more power into the solar plexus, which stimulates the immune system. He recommended that the patient listen to this music every day. The family also followed this recommendation. A few days later, the client's wife telephoned Gerhard and told him that the unpleasant odor had disappeared the day after Gerhard's visit. She also said that her husband had seemed to suffer less pain and then had died very peacefully. Later, in a conversation with the client's doctor, he confirmed that he was familiar with the smell of this particular cancer and that it was impossible to remove this odor. The doctor was astonished that the odor had disappeared.

Sometimes, the house examinations would yield humorous experiences. Gerhard was once called to examine a house. The husband was particularly interested in the bedroom and placement of the bed. He requested that Gerhard check those points very carefully. Gerhard examined the house inside and outside, going into all the rooms with his dowsing rods. At the husband's insistence, he gave a bit of extra attention to the master bedroom and placement of the bed. He determined that the bed was in a very good place and that nothing negative could be found. He discussed his examination with the couple, stating that he didn't believe it was necessary to relocate their bed or make any changes.

The woman was pleased that all was in order with her home, but her husband didn't seem contented at all. Finally, as Gerhard was leaving, the man followed him to his car while his wife remained in the house. As Gerhard prepared to drive away, the man blurted out, "I thought there must be something wrong with the location of the bed or that it could be earth radiation and that you could do something. But it isn't, so what can I do? What can I do to have a happier love life with my wife?" Gerhard shrugged his shoulders as he related this tale. If the solution to that problem could be found by dowsing, Gerhard hadn't learned it yet!

Crib Death Thirty-Six Years Later

There were also tragic and mysterious events. In August 1986, during a thunderstorm, a six-month-old baby boy had suffered a crib death in a farmhouse. A few months later, the grieving young mother contacted Gerhard and asked him to check the house for harmful earth radiation or some other condition that could have possibly caused her baby's death. She was griefstricken and desperately wanted an explanation for her loss.

He performed a house examination, including the surrounding land, and drew all the points onto a floor plan. After the house inspection, the young woman and her mother-in-law sat at the kitchen table while Gerhard explained what he had found. He had discovered water lines, Hartmann Grids, and Curry grids, all converging at the same point in the middle of the house. The child's deathbed had been positioned directly over that point!

While studying the plan, Gerhard was suddenly inspired to ask a question. "Has this house ever been struck by lightning?"

The young woman replied, "I don't know. This farm is owned by my husband's family, and I haven't lived here very long."

The mother-in-law, however, quickly responded, "Yes, indeed … lightning did strike the house at that very point many years ago. I remember it well."

She went on to explain, "There was a thunderstorm in August 1950, when my son was only three or four years old. I remember that the house was full of refugees from eastern Germany and eastern Europe. Because the house was so crowded, our son was sleeping with us. During the storm, there was a lightning strike, and he stopped breathing! There was a lot of panic and crying for help and running about. One of the refugees who knew first aid rushed over, grabbed my son, and dunked him into a nearby tub of water. This started him breathing again, and thanks to that dunking and the grace of God, he recovered.

"Later that day, someone in the room suddenly pointed up to the ceiling, and we all saw it. A black cross was seen on the ceiling of the bedroom. That cross was created by the smoke from the lightning strike. The cross had the appearance of a funeral cross and was directly on the spot where lightning had entered."

This strange event had not been forgotten, but the ceiling had been painted and repainted over the years, and the sleeping arrangements had changed often. No one had thought of it for years until Gerhard asked if the house had ever been struck by lightning. The same room was still being used as a bedroom, and the infant who had died had been lying in this room in August 1986, directly under that part of the ceiling that had been marked by lightning thirty-six years earlier in August 1950. Needless to say, the family will not have a bed in this particular place anymore.

Gerhard doesn't try to explain everything. Sometimes he just says, "It's curious."

During his dowsing activities, he met a lot of people who were suffering greatly. He wanted to help them, and he had the feeling that he could do just that. They had certainly not been helped by "normal" or traditional medicine. German citizens have access to the finest medical care, and no one needs to suffer bad health for lack of funds.

Gerhard thought about studying and becoming a naturopath or a doctor, but he knew that it would take a long time and a great deal of money. Since he had obligations like a wife, house, and business, this didn't seem like something he could readily undertake. As he was to learn, he was meant to be a healer.

Healing and Astrology

In July 1987, he met a woman who was heavily involved with the esoteric scene in Germany. She was in the health-care business and very much involved in alternative medicine and past life regressions. She asked him if he would accompany her to a natural healing congress in Essen, in the Ruhrgebiet. There, he encountered all kinds of alternative healing and new ideas. This was the beginning of his progression from an interested observer to an active participant in metaphysical activities.

In February 1989, he attended a workshop in astrology, for which he also found a natural talent. He finds the lessons of astrology very useful in his personal life but doesn't consult his horoscope to make daily decisions. He does use it as a focus for his intuition and to satisfy his curiousity about events in his life and the lives of others around him. He doesn't feel particularly gifted in astrology and certainly hasn't felt guided in this pursuit.

It was about the time of the astrology workshop that he heard of another dowsing workshop being offered. He felt that this workshop would enhance his knowledge, and he could hardly wait to take part in the next phase of his education.

In April, he attended the workshop and again was a star pupil, soaking up everything he heard and thinking very deeply about some new things. He noticed that most of the people he met at this workshop were very spiritual and that spirituality seemed to be an important element of holistic medicine. He felt like everyone in the group seemed to know more than he did, but he was learning fast and seemed to have a natural talent.

It was in this workshop that he first made the acquaintance of Hans, who would become a close associate and friend. Gerhard joined a group of Austrians, including Hans, who were very interested in metaphysics. He took part in trips, experiments, and explorations with this group, which was, in effect, a parapsychology research group. They were interested in all the new developments in alternative healing methods, including spiritual healing, energy healing, and the new field of quantum healing.

Hans lives near Salzburg and has read widely on metaphysics. He became Gerhard's tutor and mentor on many esoteric aspects. He and Hans became very close friends and companions at conferences all over Europe.

These Austrian friends conducted seminars in spiritual healing. The group had access to small offices, where they conducted their healing sesssions. After Gerhard joined this group, he plunged into personal research and experimentation. The Austrians were doing things that Gerhard hadn't imagined before, and he was hooked.

Far from forming an all-encompassing philosophy, Gerhard is still questioning, seeking, and wondering. His spirit of discovery and experimentation leads him to pose questions to doctors and scientists who seek to examine and explain his gift. He is always open to explore his abilities and is the first to question and wonder at the meaning of some new phenomena.

It was also immediately apparent that Gerhard had a gift for discovering blockages in energy flows and the role of chakras in human health. He had developed his dowsing abilities and was able to place his hands into a person's aura and discover the reasons for disfunction and illness.

4

Meeting Tom Johanson

Everything flows and nothing abides, everything
gives way and nothing stays fixed.

—Heraclitus

IN JULY 1988, THE Austrian group invited Gerhard to
accompany them to a workshop conducted by Tom
Johanson, a well-known and successful spiritualist healer
from Great Britain. Tom also enjoyed a large following in
Austria and Germany. The workshop was being held in
Hallein, Austria, so Gerhard and Hans drove there together.
It turned out to be an important turning point for Gerhard,
and he had his first experience as a healer.

There were more than one hundred people waiting
to see Tom at City Hall, where the workshop was being
held. Gerhard had expected a man with a guru-like personality, perhaps wearing a robe and heavy pendant and
speaking in mystic tones. What he did meet was a typical
English gentleman, very well dressed in stylish clothing
and Italian shoes! He wore a classic blue blazer with gold
buttons. Gerhard was impressed with this very elegant and

distinguished-looking man with a full head of beautiful, white hair. He was struck by his bright eyes, twinkling with humor and charm.

Spiritual healing was the subject, and the first thing he told the group was that it was very, very easy to become a healer. Tom stated that it took only ten minutes to learn everything one needed to know about healing energy. For the brain to absorb and accept this information, however, more proof was required, and it would take at least an entire weekend to assimilate it! Tom talked of his personal philosophy and gave some examples of healing from the Bible. His lecture was filled with humor, and Gerhard had the impression that Tom was healing and teaching with his entire capacity for love. His love radiated into the audience. Gerhard felt that everyone was as deeply touched as he was by this great outpouring of love from the speaker.

Finally, on Sunday evening, just one and a half hours before the end of the seminar, Tom said, "Now, let's do some spiritual healing. Will all the people who have problems with their shoulders and who cannot bring their hands together over their heads please stand up?"

About twenty-five people from the audience stood up. Then, Tom asked those who had remained seated to become healers for the ones standing. The healers were to close their eyes and ask for healing energy and then see what happened. Gerhard closed his eyes and asked for healing energy. At that same moment, he felt as if someone had suddenly placed very hot coins into the palms of his hands, and he could feel perspiration in his palms.

Tom then asked them to all say a small silent prayer. A few minutes later, Tom said, "OK, let's see what has happened."

He told the people who were standing to try to raise their arms over their heads. Gerhard was astonished to see that they could now move their arms quite freely! It seemed to be a miracle, and he had actually taken part in it! This was too much for Gerhard to accept, and he dismissed it immediately as a placebo effect..

Then Tom asked that all the people who couldn't move their necks to please stand up. About twenty to twenty-five people stood up, and the procedure was repeated. Gerhard had the same feeling again—as if hot coins had been placed in his hands. And again, the people who couldn't move their necks before were able to turn their heads from side to side and were seemingly healed.

Tom asked if anyone in the room had not experienced the healing energy.

An elderly lady stood up and said, "I didn't feel anything. I'm using crutches because I have problems with my right leg, and I can't move without pain."

Tom asked then for all the people in the room to become healers for this lady and to send healing energy to her. Again, Gerhard asked for the energy in his hands, felt the sensation of heat as it came into both hands— stronger than before—and mentally directed the healing energy to the woman. Amazingly, she then stood without her crutches and walked about. She was not only walking— she was dancing, laughing, and crying, all at the same time. She appeared so joyful that Gerhard was filled with happiness and wonder. He felt that he had witnessed something unusual and wonderful.

On the return trip that evening, both he and Hans were so totally charged up and full of their new experiences that they could talk of nothing else.

Gerhard's First Healing Experience

He returned to work the next day at the German Patent Office, but the experiences at the healing workshop were still very much on his mind. As he finished a research project, he found that he needed some copies of his findings. He gathered his books and went to the copy room, where he found the woman who had charge of the copy machines. When he saw her, it was obvious that she had contracted a terrible headcold over the weekend. Her eyes were red and watery, and she was sniffling.

Gerhard inquired, "Aren't you feeling well today?"

She answered that she felt just terrible. Impulsively, he remarked that he had taken part in a spiritual healing workshop over the weekend and that he could try to heal her. He was very curious to see if he could feel this healing energy and repeat the weekend experiences away from the workshop environment and Tom Johanson's presence.

When she responded, "Why not?" he was momentarily a bit flustered. Tom Johanson had taught them that they should put their hands on the part that was causing the pain, but Gerhard didn't feel comfortable in putting his hands on her face. Nevertheless, he asked her to be seated on a chair and told her he would ask for healing energy. He closed his eyes, asked for the healing energy, and said a small prayer. Instantly, he felt the sensation of heat in his hands again. He decided that he would place his hands on her face after all. However, as his hands came within a few inches of her face, they stopped on their own. There seemed to be a force that stopped his hands. He just couldn't come any closer. When he took his hands away, he noticed that red circles had appeared around her eyes as if she were wearing sunglasses.

He promised to come back in an hour to pick up his copies and see how she was doing. Upon his return, he saw that she looked enormously improved.

"How are you feeling?" he inquired.

"Oh, I'm fine," was the response, "but now I'm a little bit irritated."

"But why? Aren't you feeling better?" asked Gerhard.

"Well," she responded, "I'd planned to leave at lunch-time to see a doctor. I hoped he would write me up on sick leave for the rest of the week. Now I can't do that! After you were here, I had a runny nose for a little while, then it stopped suddenly. Since that time, I have had no problems...I'm fine now, and I'll have to work all week."

They both laughed. This was Gerhard's first personal healing experience.

A very important change occurred in Gerhard's life when he visited London for the first time in 1989. The workshop by Tom Johanson that he'd attended in Austria had been organized by a Swiss group from Zurich. The same workshop was now scheduled with Tom Johanson in London. Gerhard wanted to learn more, so he invited some friends to come to London with him. He thought that the workshop might have a different quality in London, and he was right.

This time, the energy had a different, much stronger feeling than in Austria. The area and the people made the difference, and he was excited by the atmosphere. He also saw a spiritual medium for the first time. Hermann had told him that they would be meeting mediums in London, but at that time, Gerhard wasn't particularly interested in mediumship. He didn't even believe that it was possible to have contact with persons who had died.

He had traveled to London with his friends Hermann and Hans and some others from Lubeck. They were a small group, and he'd shown them London and brought them into contact with spiritual healers who worked with the Spiritual Association of Great Britain (SAGB). The group attended an impressive mediumship demonstration there conducted by John Graham. Gerhard still wasn't convinced; he just thought it was interesting and a bit puzzling on this first visit to the SAGB. He later developed a strong personal friendship with John Graham and became a great admirer of his abilities.

Tom Johanson's Wife Was Also a Medium

One evening, Tom's wife, Coral Polge-Johanson, joined Tom in the healing circle. She was also a medium, but her mediumship was definitely different from any other mediums Gerhard had seen thus far on this visit. Like most mediums, she claimed to have a guide. That guide was ostensibly Maurice de la Tour, a French painter from the seventeenth century. Coral was a gifted artist herself, and her mediumship took the form of creating paintings of departed souls or their spirit guides. These paintings or drawings, when compared with actual photographs or portraits, were amazingly accurate.

That evening, she took a seat in front of the group and began. She had a drawing board beside her. She did a short meditation for about half a minute. Then she began to paint.

In a few minutes, she had drawn the face of a person. She was talking all the time she was painting. She said that she had the spirit of a person with her, a small person who was a mother and grandmother. Coral described the woman and said that she was talking about cooking, or it could be that she owned a pub or something, but there was a connection with cooking. She said she had a unique pair of earrings. She asked if anyone in the group knew who this person might be.

A man from Gerhard's group stood up and said, "That's my grandmother. We lived in Switzerland, and she owned a pub."

The medium then asked, "What's with the earrings and the other jewelry?"

The man was astonished at this question because when his grandmother died, they had discovered that all of her jewelry had disappeared. No one in the family knew where it was, apparently including the grandmother! This was very surprising to Gerhard because he knew that Mrs. Johanson had never before seen this man—and she knew about his grandmother and her missing jewelry.

Gerhard Visits a Medium

After this experience, Gerhard decided that he would try to arrange a personal appointment with a medium, just to see what would happen. He went to the offices of the SAGB in London's Berwick Square, which was only ten minutes from his hotel. There, he got the name and address of a medium named Evelyn Payne.

Before, when he thought of a medium, he imagined an old woman with a shawl over her shoulders, a crystal ball, and dark lighting. She might use tarot cards or a crystal ball to tell him who he would meet or marry, when he would die, and so on. With this preconception, he went to see Evelyn Payne. When he arrived, he was shown to a small room, where the medium was waiting for him. No shawl, no gold earrings, no long skirt, no crystal ball. She looked like an average English lady, possibly in her early sixties. She was very smartly dressed and looked more like a bank executive than a medium.

"Come in," she said, and began almost immediately. "I see a man who is standing behind you. He is not as tall as you, but a gentleman with thick, coarse hair and a mustache. He stands very straight and his name is Andrew."

"That's my grandfather!" Gerhard exclaimed.

She went on, "He's so glad to be with you."

Gerhard then told her that his grandfather had died in 1956.

She said, "Yes, and since then he's been working with you—he brings you into contact with people who are important for you to do your work in this life."

Gerhard thought about that. He recalled a lot of important events in his life, which had seemed random, and saw that they exhibited a pattern unfolding. In 1967, he'd come to the German Patent Office almost as if by accident. Also, seemingly by accident, he'd started a career in patent and trademark research. And he'd met a lot of people who changed his life, again by accident.

The medium also told him that his grandfather loved to travel but hadn't had the opportunity while he was alive, so now he traveled everywhere with Gerhard and helped him to meet the right people.

Evelyn went on to tell him that there was another gentleman with him who was one of his spiritual guides. He wasn't a member of Gerhard's family, but they had been together in a past life in ancient Greece, when they were both healers in the Temple of Music. When Gerhard heard that, he was speechless. Although he had never seen this lady before in his life, she had just alluded to Gerhard's use of music in his healing sessions.

This medium didn't know and couldn't know that he was working as a healer. She also couldn't know that he had just begun to use music in his private healings. In fact, no one knew about it except Gerhard and the people he'd worked with privately. He hadn't yet introduced the concept of healing with music at his seminars.

Evelyn then told him that this Greek healer guides and helps him and that it would be helpful for him to listen to harp music. Even as a young child, Gerhard had especially enjoyed harp music. At this point, he confirmed to Evelyn that he was interested in spiritual healing. She told him that it would be very important for him and that healing was his true life's work.

When she told him about the ancient Greek guide, he understood and accepted it immediately. He remembered that when he was learning about the history of ancient

Greece in school, he hadn't needed to study it to learn it—he already knew it. He would read the page and somehow recognize it—he would remember it as if he'd experienced it. Conversely, even though he'd been born and raised in Germany, he'd had a lot of difficulty in learning German history, especially the history of the sixteenth century. That period had been like a blackout for him.

After his meeting with Evelyn, Gerhard felt more strongly that he could accept and agree with spiritualism and spiritual guidance in our lives. He has often felt the presence of his grandfather, and the medium confirmed the influence in his life.

Both Tom and his wife, Coral, have since passed over to the other side. They both had a significant influence on Gerhard and the development of his own spiritual healing abilities.

Meeting John Graham and Attending a Mediumship Demonstration at the SAGB

On his first trip to London, Gerhard had met John Graham at a demonstration sponsored by the SAGB, and that proved to be a very important meeting for him. He found himself seated next to John at the hotel, and they struck up a conversation about a book John was reading. As they talked, they seemed to find many things to connect them. Gerhard promised to send him some classical music recordings from Germany. After that, Gerhard always met with John whenever he visited London. On this latest trip, Gerhard had gotten to know John Graham a lot better, and a close friendship had formed.

Whenever he came to London, Gerhard always visited the mediumship demonstrations in the rooms of the SAGB. These demonstrations are open to the public for a nominal fee, and Gerhard found them quite interesting. At one such demonstration, most of the people in the room appeared to be from London. A medium stood at the front of the room, and she seemed to be on target with her messages to the audience.

She said to a man in the audience, "I have a message for you. There's a man—a tall man—and he was a carpenter. But he had a . . . he died by an accident. He fell down and hit his head."

The man responded, "That's my father—he died six years ago."

She went on, "Your father shows me a ticket—are you planning a journey?"

"Yes we are; we think we'll start a journey to Palestine."

"Do this. Do this," she said. "It's very important for you."

Then, the medium turned toward Gerhard and spoke directly to him.

"Your parents are here, and they're very proud of what you're doing. You are a healer, and you will go into hospitals to heal people."

She continued, "And you'll go over the great water."

He managed to thank her for this startling bit of information. He was gratified to hear that his parents approved of his healing, but he wondered what she meant by "going over the great water." Years later, he remembered her words when he purchased his first airline ticket to travel to the United States.

During his next trip to London, Gerhard and his wife were accompanied by Hans and his wife, Marlene. Hans and Marlene were from Salzburg and were part of the Austrian group that had been so important to Gerhard's development. They visited another mediumship demonstration, and the four of them were seated together in a row. The medium spoke to Marlene and told her that there was a gentleman there who'd always had a headache on his right side.

"He's a very tall man," she said. "Who is this?"

Marlene said, "That's my father—he had this problem."

The medium continued to report that a little boy was standing beside her father and that his name was Peter. Tears sprang to Marlene's eyes, and it became very difficult for her to answer. She had lost a baby boy by a miscarriage. They had decided to give him the name Peter. It was apparent that the medium had contact with Marlene's father and her child. This was a very touching and evidential moment for all of them.

This experience gave Gerhard a lot of trust in mediumship, but only at this high level of quality. There are many persons who call themselves mediums and offer readings to the public. Among them are a few charlatans and swindlers. Some of these people might genuinely feel they are in contact with deceased persons. The swindlers and well-intentioned persons alike might be very good at providing generic messages and platitudes that might be accepted as genuine by a person who is yearning for a meaningful message. The proof, however, is in the message itself. A specific reference to a subject which could only be known to the decedent and the person getting the message is evidence of a genuine contact. A generic message that the mother is happy on the other side and is often watching the family may give comfort to the person getting the reading, but it is not a proof of survival of the spirit.

Gerhard Begins to Receive Messages While Healing

When Gerhard came home from this London trip, he had more experiences with auras. He found that he could put his hands in the aura and he could feel pain or blockages. He could feel the energy flowing. When he started the seminars, a central part of the workshop involved asking for volunteers for an aura reading. He would demonstrate his technique of feeling their auras and sharing his impressions of their health problems. He would demonstrate how he found the problems and how they could be treated. After his return from this trip to London, he was holding a seminar with a small group. A friend asked him to feel her aura. As he raised his hands to begin, he suddenly smelled the aroma of hops.

He asked, "Do you have a relationship or link to a person who worked with hops?"

She responded, "Yes—my granduncle. He was a hops dealer."

His eyes closed, Gerhard inquired, "Was your granduncle a small man who took great care of his clothing and wardrobe? Could it be that he ironed his shirts by himself because his wife couldn't iron the cuffs to his satisfaction?"

"Yes," she confirmed, "this is exactly how he was."

"And could it be that he was a prisoner of war in Russia and he didn't come home until 1954?"

"Yes, that's true."

Then Gerhard saw an image of birdcages in this man's living room.

"He says he would never have caged birds again because birds sing much more beautifully outside than inside."

She responded, "Yes, he had caged birds, which he had caught himself. He told us before he died that he regretted having caged the birds."

At the same moment, Gerhard saw a girl who questioned if the lady was drinking enough water. He passed the question on. "Do you drink enough water?"

She replied, "Yes, you're right. I should drink more water because I have a kidney problem."

This is an example of a reading with specific information that was unknown to the medium at the time of the reading and one of Gerhard's first mediumship experiences.

Now, it is not uncommon for him to receive messages while he is working. Although he was well acquainted with his friend, he was not aware that her deceased grand uncle was a hops broker and had kept caged birds. This is what is meant by quality information.

After Gerhard began to conduct his own seminars, he noticed that he could feel the patterns of past lives. He describes this as a very cold feeling, something like a cold shower, coming over him at the moment a spirit enters. He is never afraid but feels a great respect for what he is experiencing. At that moment, he says that his thoughts are very, very clear. This effect only occurs when he is in contact with a spirit.

A Message to the Medium from Gerhard

During one of Gerhard's trips to London, he and John Graham visited a demonstration by a lady and young man who were mediums. Suddenly, while watching the medium, Gerhard saw a taller man, standing very straight and serious, behind the young man. The tall man was looking intently at his shoes, which were bright brown and shone like mirrors! After the demonstration, Gerhard asked the young man if he knew the gentleman who was standing behind him.

"Yes," he replied, "he was my grandfather, who retired from service in the British Army. He always shined his shoes himself and took pride in shining his shoes and lining them up neatly in a row!"

Gerhard was happy and pleased to have this confirmation of what he had seen.

Gerhard attended three of Tom Johanson's seminars in London. Tom's wife, Coral, died in 2001 and Tom followed her in 2002. Tom had Alzheimer's and he was already quite old when Gerhard knew him. On each visit to London, Gerhard saw his friend and fellow healer, John Graham.

He came to London with all his friends and got to know John and got to know London. Gerhard is so familiar with London that he feels he could be a tour guide. Due to the closeness of this relationship with John, he learned more about mediumship.

An American's Concerns About Castle Fortifications

Michael first met Gerhard at a demonstration party in Tucson, Arizona. Gerhard sometimes conducts demonstrations of his healing abilities in private homes in a very informal atmosphere. This particular evening was unusual in that most of the guests were in the medical or health services fields. No one was skeptical or cynical, and almost everyone was open to alternative healing and especially spiritual healing. Although Gerhard had conducted an all-day workshop in Tucson and had just had time for a quick sandwich for dinner, he slipped into the healing mode quite easily and proceeded to conduct demonstration healings for the guests present. One by one, they stood before him for a quick reading and some remarkable results. Everyone seemed to be astonished at what was happening.

Finally, very late in the evening, a tall and handsome man named Michael stepped forward for a healing. The following is his own written account of what happened next.

When it came my turn, his opening question to me when he felt my aura was did I have a concern about castles, which, of course, is not a very off-the-cuff remark that you might make to anybody. Curiously enough, I have always been fascinated with castles and am very intrigued with their defenses and their fortifications; how do you attack a castle, how do you defend one, and whenever I have visited castles in

Europe, and I've visited hundreds, I have always had a sense of knowing where things are.

I was always drawn to specific types of castles which would be more feudal and which would be involved in a time of siege. I was drawn to the parapets and to particular areas of defense known as mutriahs and michocoleen. These are firing points. We had just returned from Europe about four months prior to meeting Gerhard where once again we spent a lot of time in France and visited a number of castles and I was the only one in our group that wanted to go visit these castles. The others wanted to go sightseeing and shopping. But I wanted to explore the castles and explore the fortifications. So, when Gerhard asked me the question, it almost knocked me off my feet because this had been my secret passion my whole life of understanding these. But whenever I visited the castles, I would stand up on these parapets and I would look through the michocoleen and mutriahs and I would look at the firing point and I would get the sense of who could shoot at me. A sense of what it was like, of someone shooting at me. So when Gerhard said that I had been shot from above and he removed the projectile, it just felt completely natural and right.

Michael always suspected that his interest in castles went back to a previous life but hadn't known that he was carrying a projectile, probably an arrow, with him for the past few hundred years. Michael handed me a cassette tape with this account, and it was necessary for me to research castle defense and fortifications to discover the correct spelling of michocoleen and mutriahs. I am not able to answer any other questions on this topic. This was Michael's validation of his reading experience.

Messages from the Other Side

It's not unusual for Gerhard to get symbols and messages while he's working with people. Sometimes during the surgery and healings, he feels guided to channel messages from spirit guides or friends and relatives in the spirit world. His primary focus and direction, however, is on diagnosis and healing in the aura. Most of his messages will focus on the body and what is going on with the energy. If, for example, he sees a snake coiled in the aura, it might signify that the person died of snakebite in a previous life. He will then test in the aura for symptoms of poisoning. If the results are positive for venom, he will treat that condition. In cases like that, he will generally use a syringe to inject an antivenom. The resulting cure can be quite dramatic for one who has suffered a lifetime of unexplained pain.

5

The Power of Music

Music gives a soul to the universe, wings to the
mind, flight to the imagination and life to everything.

—Plato

THE MARCH 31, 2002, issue of *Parade* magazine contained an article relating to the healing power of music.
Two leading proponents of the healing power of music are
Connie Tomaino, director of the Institute of Music and
Neurologic Function, and Dr. Oliver Sachs, neurologist and
author of the book, *Awakenings*, which was made into a
feature film starring Robin Williams. Dr. Sachs wrote of
"frozen" patients who had been literally unable to move,
some for many years, due to a sleeping sickness. The effects
of music on these patients was surprising, dramatic, and
scientifically proven by the EKGs! Dr. Sachs discovered
that music brought the sufferer out of the frozen state to
an animated and interested one. When the patient participated by singing or playing an instrument, the effect
was even more dramatic. Of course, the music had to "fit"

the patient. It had to evoke emotion and response in the individual. Music is personal. Some people like classical music, while others resonate with popular music or rock and roll. Conversely, some kinds of music are more conducive to disharmony than harmony, evoking dark images and negative feelings. This kind of music would have an opposite effect—sickening rather than healing.

In short, responsiveness to music is hardwired to our psyche. It is easy to imagine that the entire universe is pulsating with a song to which we are able to respond with the deepest emotions.

Gerhard understands himself as a channel for cosmic energies and works with a number of spirit guides skilled in a large variety of techniques. Music plays a large part in this process. Participants are told to listen to music (mostly classical) during meditation and direct this music and energy to the ailing body parts. He personally estimates that he is able to help about 86 percent of the people he sees. After his first visit to America, at least two of his clients were able to cancel previously scheduled surgeries after their medical doctors verified that the problem had disappeared.

One patient actually reported to the hospital for a scheduled surgery and was sent home when the tumor could not be seen on the new X-rays. Another client, who had been diagnosed with an inoperable brain tumor, reported back to her friends in Tucson that the tumor disappeared. (There will be more information on this particular case later.)

Musicosophia

During the fall of 1988 and spring of 1989, Gerhard took part in three very interesting workshops known as Musicosophia. The Musicosophia concept was founded by George Balan, a Romanian-born music professor who fled the country in 1977 in order to pursue a spiritual approach to music. At that time, of course, Romania was a Communist controlled dictatorship. Balan has published countless books on music that have been translated into many languages. Balan founded a school, the first one to develop the ability to listen to and appreciate music on many levels. The workshops are based on a philosophy concerning the tones and frequencies of classical music. The school also offers a three-year plan of study which can be completed in Germany, Italy, Spain, or Mexico. No musical abilities or knowledge of an instrument is necessary to enroll in these classes. A main feature of this concept is that by moving the hands and forming the music, harmony will be brought to the mind, body, and spirit. Listening to music in this fashion makes it a much more intense and meaningful experience for the listener. One needs to hear it for only a few moments to drift into a meditative state because the music and movements bring harmony to the body and soul.

Gerhard had always loved music, but the workshops were very special indeed. Since that time, he listens to music with, as he says, "different ears." In one of these workshops which was held in Austria, Gerhard first experienced the music of Gustav Mahler. Mahler's *Symphony Number One*, which was the selection for that workshop. That evening and well into the night, the music kept running through his waking moments and also in his dreams. When he returned home, he immediately went to a music store to find recordings of this music and began to work it into his own seminars.

He found that this kind of meditation was something he could use. He had participated in many workshops where everyone would sit in a lotus position, not moving, for hours, or try to concentrate on a single point and try to remove all thoughts from the mind. Unfortunately, that kind of meditation was never productive for Gerhard. With music, however, something wonderful happened. He could listen to music and achieve a meditative and peaceful state. Best of all, he discovered that by moving his hands to the music, he could bring the vibration of the music into his body and be able to feel it with his entire being. He was captivated with and carried by the music.

He meditated to the Coronation Concert of Mozart, Piano Concert no. 26, Second Movement, which was only four and a half minutes long. After he had heard the music several times, he found that he could close his eyes and hear the first tone. Then, in his brain, he would hear the music as if it were playing on a disc. He perceived that there seemed to be ten to twenty seconds difference in the music, depending on whether he listened with his eyes open or closed, or sitting down or standing up. It was curious about the duration of the music seeming different to him because he felt the vibration of the music in his body and felt in total harmony with the music. Gerhard spoke of the music as being his mantra throughout the day. Even while he was engaged in other pursuits and not listening, the music continued to resonate and bring harmony to his being.

While attending the Musicosophia workshop for his favorite composer, Gustav Mahler, he had the experience of feeling his own aura for the first time. The others in the workshop were watching the wall, where projected lights were dancing with the melody, but Gerhard closed his eyes and listened to the movement while moving his hands. Suddenly, he felt something very unusual and different when he moved his hands in front of his face!

It was like an energy, an electricity, especially when he moved his hand in front of the area where the third eye is supposedly located. And he knew what it was at that moment because he had learned about the aura during the seminars. He was naturally very excited to discover that he could actually feel his own aura. This was a major development in unlocking his newfound abilities.

He was so filled with excitement at this new feeling that he had to share it with a friend who lived in Regensburg. She was a natural healer, and he went to see her to tell her about this new experience. He was having so much trouble describing it that he decided to try to show her by giving her the same experience.

He asked her to sit down while the music played, and he used his hands to bring the energy into her aura. When the music stopped, he asked her what she felt.

Her response was, "Oh, I feel like an energy in my hands. It's tingling all around me—everything is tingling."

The Healing Power of Music

Music is the the language of the soul. It speaks to us in more ways than we think. In the depths of our hearts—in our innermost feelings—music answers a longing for love and peace. When we listen to music with our hearts as well as our ears, it can stir our emotions and our responses.

It can be classical music, but it can also be popular or folk music that has the power to move us emotionally in ways that we can only begin to understand on a conscious level.

During the workshops, Gerhard demonstrates different ways of listening to music. If you listen to music on a purely intellectual level, or just with your ears, you will enjoy the sound, but it will not reach your heart. On a purely analytical basis, you can appreciate the tone, the quality of the violins, trumpets, pianos, or all the instruments playing in unison to create a perfect work. However, if you will listen to the music and move your arms and hands with the rhythm, you may begin to hear the music with a different level of understanding. The body then becomes a part of the symphony. By doing this, the music will reach the heart and touch that center, where love is said to reside. In this way, we come nearer to the inner music of our own hearts and awaken a true love for ourselves and recognition of ourselves as eternal beings in harmony with the universe...

Spiritual healing is healing that works through the power of love. Music helps us to discover this healing energy for ourselves and also for our fellow beings.

Music is also felt in our auras. During the workshops, each person learns to feel and experience his or her own aura and also the auras of other persons. Through music, the energy from the heart will raise the energy in the hands. This energy can be seen as light that streams from the fingertips. Participants learn how to clean the aura with music and, through various exercises, experience being "carried" by music.

Moving with music allows one to rediscover inner peace and freedom from everyday worries. After a two-day workshop, people report feeling as if they've just returned from a week's vacation.

Gerhard says, "With music, I try to give everybody the total and complete feeling of seeing themselves and their environment through love, as part of a universe that knows no boundaries."

Michael Newton, PhD, has this to say about music in his book, *Destiny of Souls*:

From my research, I have come to believe that more than any other medium, music uplifts the soul with ranges of notes far beyond what we know on Earth. There seems to be no limit to the sounds used in the creation of music in the spirit world. People in deep hypnosis explain that musical thought is the language of souls. The composition and transmission of harmonic resonance appears to relate to the formation and presentation of spiritual language. Far beyond musical communication, I'm told spiritual harmonics are the building blocks of energy creation and soul unification.

A Google search of the words healing and music provided one hundred fifty-nine million results at the time of this writing!

An additional hobby for Gerhard—sometimes he's a popular deejay at a local clubs or parties!

6

The Seminars Begin

Happiness is neither within us only, nor without us; it is the union of ourselves with God.

—Blaise Pascal

GERHARD WANTED TO SHARE the experience of feeling the aura with others in his seminars. He wanted to bring this experience to more people just to see what would happen. He did his first workshop in October 1988 for a week. Just two couples attended. The title of that seminar was "Healing with Color, Forms, and Music." He was well prepared with videos, an overhead projector, lots of material, and lots of ideas. He planned to conduct the workshop outdoors because it was being held in a beautiful Alpine resort area in Austria. He could hardly wait to experience the music in this beautiful environment.

As luck would have it, though, it rained the entire week, and everything had to be done inside. But every day was wonderful! Every day was filled with fun and music. At the end of the seminar, he looked at the material he hadn't used and thought he could continue for another week. The participants were all thrilled with their experiences, and so was he. For a long time after that, he received holiday cards from these couples. They always reminded him how much they had enjoyed this musical and magical workshop. The workshop was a positive experience for him and participants alike.

He began to do more and more seminars. He thought he needed help in organizing the seminars, and he found Ulli. She lived in Munich and helped him organize short demonstrations and weekend workshops in different locations in Bavaria. Her contacts helped him to establish a reputation and keep him busy on weekends and vacations, which was the only time he could spare away from his occupation. Each seminar had the same theme, but each one was different.

Planning a Seminar

When he first had the idea to conduct a seminar, he didn't know what would happen. Gerhard never makes more than a rough plan for a seminar. He knows how it will begin but doesn't know how it will proceed. He knows the first piece of music when he begins the seminar. After that, each unfolds according to spiritual guidance, through hearing and feeling the music. The spiritual events occur and unfold as the music is selected and played. Each seminar is a learning experience which is useful in planning future seminars. The seminars are exciting and sometimes new themes are discovered. They provide an opportunity for participants to enjoy new experiences and share new ideas with one another. Every seminar brings a new set of participants who have different experiences and different mindsets.

The seminars may not be comfortable for all people. If people are open to new ideas and experiences, they are welcome. Although Gerhard has occasionally been asked to conduct specific types of seminars for special interests or groups, he doesn't feel he should change what he does to suit an audience.

Meeting Hermann

Hermann lives in Lubeck, a town in northern Germany. Gerhard first met him during an astrology workshop in Munich. They were introduced to one another and discovered that they shared an interest in airplanes. When Hermann found that Gerhard possessed a great deal of information about airplanes of the Second World War, he besieged him with questions about this passion. Gerhard has had this interest since he was a young boy and laughs that one of the major disappointments of his young life occurred when he discovered that he couldn't join the United States Air Force. That was his only goal as a small boy! He had no interest in joining the Luftwaffe, the German Air Force. The reason for this lack of interest in joining the Luftwaffe lay in his immediate past life, but that story will be related later.

Gerhard was particularly interested in the development and construction of jet airplanes during the Second World War. Later, Gerhard discovered that Hermann suspected a karmic tie and knew a great deal about reincarnation. In fact, Hermann is an accomplished hypnotist and is able to help Gerhard recover memories of his past lives. This skill has enabled Gerhard to understand and develop his gift of healing.

When Gerhard first got to know Hermann, he thought it was curious that Hermann was always talking about reincarnation and his past lives and all the catastrophes he had suffered in past lives. Whenever Hermann saw people with difficulties, he would ask if they had some experience in a past life to explain the current life problem. Curious about Hermann's passionate interest, Gerhard began to read about reincarnation, and it seemed very interesting and logical to him. He thought perhaps he should learn more about this subject.

This friendship ripened, and Hermann became very interested in Gerhard's spiritual healing seminars. He invited Gerhard to come to northern Germany and offered to help him do seminars in Lubeck. Thus, Gerhard was introduced to yet another circle of friends and supporters.

Hermann Helps With Workshops

Gerhard's next seminar in Lubeck was conducted in a teacher-student dynamic. Gerhard stood in front of the audience and told them about healing and explained theories to them. He had a lot of drawings and information and exhibits. He explained, and they listened, but it didn't seem to be so smooth this time—and not nearly as much fun.

Hermann said that he didn't think this was the right way. "You must be among the people," he explained. "They must feel your vibration."

So he changed the workshop atmosphere and his methods. He sat, stood, walked, and danced with the participants. He noticed immediately that the entire energy changed. It was during this next workshop that Gerhard had another new experience.

He was feeling the aura of one of the seminar participants. Suddenly and surprisingly, he received a lot of information about her grandmother, who had died one year before. When he told her what he was receiving, she confirmed that everything about her grandmother was true and felt that she had received a communication from her. This was one of his first experiences with spiritual guidance and mediumship.

Hanging in the Monastery

Gerhard conducted a workshop in a village near Landshut. The workshop room was located in an old monastery that had been renovated into a seminar center. Some very strange things had happened there, and it was rumored to be haunted.

On the first evening of the seminar, the group was seated in the dining room, waiting for dinner to be served. Ulli, the lady who helped Gerhard organize seminars, came down from her room and joined the group at the table.

Upon seating herself, she suddenly remarked, "Oh, where is the key to my room? I just had it in my hand, and I locked the door with it. It was a very large key with a holder showing the room number."

It had disappeared between her room and the dining room! It wasn't on or around the table. The doors in this hotel all required a key to lock and unlock. Some of the group walked back with her to look along the floor and up the stairs, but the key could not be found.

So, Ulli went to the desk clerk of the hotel for an extra key to open the room. The desk clerk sighed and smiled. "It's happened again?"

The desk clerk took a spare key from the wall and walked in front of Ulli and the others back to the room on the second floor. She unlocked the door and opened it wide.

Ulli gasped and pointed to the nightstand. "There it is! But I locked the door behind me when I left!"

"Yes, I know," replied the desk clerk. "This is not the first time this has happened."

They were all baffled, but the desk clerk went back downstairs to resume her duties with no further comments or explanations.

The next day during a morning meditation, a participant named Peter began to laugh. He continued to laugh all during the meditation. The entire group heard him chuckling and chortling from the back of the room.

It finally became so annoying that Gerhard stopped the

meditation and went to him and felt his aura. There was a very strong and heavy energy on his back and shoulders. He brought Peter to the center of the room and asked him to sit in a chair in front of the group. Gerhard again felt his aura and noticed that his head had dropped forward and his chin was resting almost on his chest. Gerhard made a pulling motion behind Peter. Peter's hand went to his throat, and he complained that he couldn't breathe.

Gerhard knew then that he had found a noose in Peter's aura. He sent one of the participants to the kitchen to fetch a large knife, which he used to cut the karmic rope away. Then Gerhard sensed an entity in the aura. The other participants gathered around Peter and added their energy to Gerhard's in order to release the earthbound entity. At the same moment the entity departed, Peter said that he felt lighter and relieved.

The group then went to the back of the room, where Peter had been sitting during the meditation. Gerhard noticed that the support beams on the wall behind his chair gave the appearance of a gallows!

After the entity had been released, the group was then able to finish the meditation with no further bursts of hilarity from Peter, who was now able to join them.

Later, in the dining room during lunch, one of the cooks came out and relayed a bit of history on the old monastery to the group. One of the participants then shared the story of Peter's experience during the meditation, and the cook nodded knowingly. He said that it was known that some of the monks had indeed committed suicide by hanging. The monastery was several centuries old, having existed since the early Middle Ages. The group could talk of nothing else during lunch.

More Seminars

It was at that point that Gerhard began to have problems with the authorities in Germany because spiritual healing was not allowed. Gerhard tried to continue with the healing workshops without charging money, but soon learned that was also not permitted. The German authorities simply said, "No, not allowed." Healing could only come from licensed healers. One had to study natural healing methods for three years, be tested by a professional board, and become what is known there as a heilpraktiker. We would call this a naturopath.

Since Gerhard's healing methods didn't involve herbs and vitamins and massage, and he couldn't afford to give up his full-time occupation, he ruled it out as an option to continue spiritual healing in Germany. He simply conducted his workshops outside the country. He found a ready clientele in the Netherlands, Switzerland, Austria, Denmark, Great Britain, Scotland, Spain, Italy, Finland, and the United States.

The workshops provided him an ongoing education and an ever-growing reputation. Many people have referred to Gerhard as a Wunderheiler or miracle worker. Gerhard is not comfortable with these labels. He refers to himself as an aura surgeon and is continuously seeking to understand the nature of this ability. He earnestly believes that all persons have the capacity to heal themselves, only being limited by our lack of understanding. For him, it is an ongoing process of discovery and enlightenment.

Mediumship

Mediumship is an important part of Gerhard's healing gift. There is no doubt that Gerhard is acting as a medium

71

between the spirit world and this when he allows doctors from the spirit side to work through him in the auras of patients who are living on this side. Sometimes, he receives messages from his guide about the past life of the person standing before him. Usually, they relate to the condition being treated, but sometimes it seems as if the spirit world takes the opportunity to convey other messages and information.

Reggie and Peanuts

At a workshop in southern Arizona, there was a young man that endeared himself to everyone present. Gerhard recognized him immediately as a very gifted healer himself. He seemed to be especially talented with working with women, who seemed to feel immediate empathy for him. He was a small and muscular young man and sported a couple of tattoos. He actually didn't look very spiritual to me until he smiled and I looked into his eyes, which radiated love and warmth. I myself felt very motherly toward him and observed how sensitive and empathic he seemed.

One evening, after the workshop ended, he requested a private healing session with Gerhard. It had been a long day, but Gerhard consented, and they began. It wasn't very private since the room was still filled with workshop participants, but the other participants kept a respectable distance to give them a little bit of privacy. The healing progressed with Gerhard clearing up some physical problems. As the session drew to a close, Gerhard suddenly announced that an elderly lady was present and had something to say to Reggie! This caught the attention of those who were still in the room, and we listened intently.

Gerhard felt that she was Reggie's grandmother. She then gave Gerhard some business advice, which Reggie was pleased to have. He said that he'd missed his grandmother a lot because she had always encouraged him and given him good advice while she was living. Reggie had lost some money and business due to an employee he'd trusted too much and was still trying to recover from those mistakes. She told him that she was watching over the cash end of the business now and if he would just pay attention to his intuition, she was sure she could still help him.

She then smiled and held out a bowl of peanuts to Gerhard, remarking that he should tell Reggie, "Peanuts is OK."

Upon hearing the message, Reggie laughed out loud! He explained that when his baby son was born, he gave him the nickname "Peanuts." Grandmother had been outspoken with her displeasure with this nickname. She had wanted Reggie to always call the baby by his proper birth name. Now she had found a way to tell him that she'd changed her mind.

A Conductor Appears at a Workshop

At the end of each workshop, Gerhard asks the participants to arrange themselves into a semicircle in front of him. Everyone relaxes and prepares for a very special meditation and experience. Gerhard chooses music and then he personally directs and channels the music into the auras of the people seated before him. He closes his eyes and moves his hands and arms with the music. This is very relaxing and meaningful for everybody, and the music becomes very personal when it is directed into your aura in this way.

Occasionally, however, something unexpected happens. Most of the participants only notice that Gerhard seems carried with the music. This is the only time during a workshop that Gerhard can be said to go into a trancelike state. Sometimes, a medium or clairvoyant person is seated among the participants, and then the story gets a bit more interesting.

During one of these trances in Phoenix, a lady reported to the group that she could see a funny man standing behind Gerhard, directing the music and dancing around. This man had a shock of white hair and seemed to be enjoying the music. His arms were actually encased within Gerhard's arms!

Upon hearing of the little man, Gerhard wondered if it could have been the spirit of Gustav Mahler, as he felt quite close to him and his music. He found a picture of Mahler on one of his CDs and asked the woman if this could be the man.

"No," she responded vehemently, "it wasn't him."

Suddenly, she pointed to another CD with a picture of Leonard Bernstein on the cover and said, "It was him! This is the man I saw standing behind you."

Gerhard recounts this experience as a very curious one and now offers Leonard Bernstein or other musical conductors the opportunity to direct the music at the end of each workshop. Once, he was obliged to start over, since the *director* wasn't satisfied with the music Gerhard had chosen!

There is a lot of humor in the spirit world!

The growing public attention has also brought Gerhard detractors, who set up entire web pages for the purpose of exposing him as a fraud and charlatan. Not one of the detractors has met with Gerhard or interviewed him. Gerhard welcomes honest and scientific investigations. He still has many questions about this process.

He is neither a miracle worker nor a charlatan. He's an exceptionally gifted medium who is still on the learning path.

7

Gerhard's Past Lives

Why Does He Need to Be a Healer?

What we need are a few "mad" people. Look
where "sensible" ones have got us.

　　　　　　　　　—George Bernard Shaw

GERHARD BEGAN TO DISCOVER his own past life memories.
He worked with his friend Hermann to discover past life
memories; he also experienced spontaneous recall. The following are accounts of the three most important chapters
in his life progression, which affect his life and work today.

Memories of the Wehrmacht

Although Gerhard's good friend Hermann is an amateur,
he's a gifted regression hypnotist. In 1993, Gerhard arrived
in Lubeck to spend some time with Hermann and his wife,
Renate. Hermann suggested that they make a motor trip
to Wismar and Mecklenburg in East Germany, which had
recently reunited with West Germany.

During the journey to Wismar, Gerhard had a very, very
strange feeling because of the landscape. It depressed him.

Many West Germans had never had the opportunity to visit their sister state and fellow Germans. It was during this trip that two very specific things happened that prompted past life regression therapy with Hermann.

The monotony of the landscape and drive had placed Gerhard into a semi-trance while Hermann drove.

He said to Hermann, "I feel so sad when I'm seeing this landscape."

"What kind of picture do you have with your inner eye—with your third eye?"

Gerhard replied that he had a feeling of sitting in a car, but it was a military vehicle, and he was in the uniform of the Wehrmacht, the Germany Army. "I'm on my way from Peenamunde to Berlin."

Hermann asked him, "What are you doing there?"

He was suddenly and spontaneously recalling a past life in the military. He felt he was at the wheel of a military vehicle. It was near the end of World War II, and he knew himself to be a member of the Wehrmacht. He was an officer and driver for scientists and engineers in the area around Peenamunde, the site for rocket research used by the Nazis.

He knew that he had a particularly close acquaintance with and admiration for Wernher Von Braun. In this lifetime Gerhard once saw a picture of Hermann Goering and instinctively knew that he had a handshake like a wet fish, particularly limp. Later, he read the exact same information in a book and nodded to himself. He wondered how he knew that at the time.

"I'm the direction officer for Hermann Goering and Wernher Von Braun," Gerhard said. "Normally, I have a driver, but on this day, I have no driver. I'm driving by myself, and I feel very, very depressed."

Hermann asked, "Why are you so depressed?"

Gerhard responded that he was married. He could

remember his wife's name and his own name in that lifetime.

Hermann asked Gerhard if he had any feeling that his wife was still alive.

Gerhard responded, "Yes, she's still living in London."

When Hermann asked for the names, Gerhard responded with both full names. (Since this is such a recent lifetime, the names are not being published in this book.)

This spontaneous regression and Hermann's questions brought out the following story. He and his wife were married in 1936. He knows that they had four children, one of whom was seriously ill.

Because of his aeronautical experience and interest in rocket technology, he had a great many friends and acquaintances in the Royal Air Force because all pilots and people who were involved in the construction process of airplanes were like a big family. He claims that the Germans and British enjoyed a close cooperation up to the onset of the war. Aviation and rocket science weren't respected at that time. Many people laughed at anyone who believed in such things and considered them fools.

He related that in April 1939, his wife and their little daughter became critically ill, and no one could help in Germany. His wife had taken all the children to London, where she was living with friends and getting medical help for their sick child. When the war broke out, she was unable to get back to Germany. He was separated from his family. He was totally disillusioned with the Nazi regime and was discouraged about the general state of affairs.

He recalled that it was in November 1943, and he was driving the car and having depressing thoughts about the war and his personal situation. He had the feeling that everything he believed and everything that inspired and encouraged him was in the end terribly wrong, that the Nazi regime misused his energy and his feelings. He saw no more purpose in life. He saw an Army truck coming toward the intersection, and he just didn't apply the brakes. He turned the wheel and drove into the path of a large oncoming truck with his car. He knew that this life ended there, and he recalled nothing after the wreck.

One year later, Gerhard received an invitation from John Graham, his good friend in London, to visit and take a vacation with him in Tunbridge Wells. When he arrived in Tunbridge, he says that he immediately felt he belonged there somehow and that he was at home, although he had never been there before. He did something else he had never done before. He thought of his wife in that former life and took the phone book and looked up the name he still remembered. He found it.

He couldn't sleep that whole night. There was the name in the phone book. What had even made him look for it? He'd never done that in any other city he'd visited. He wondered if he should visit her, to see where she was living, but by morning, he had decided against it. She would be quite old now and would not recognize him.

He also recognized that his appearance at her door wouldn't contribute to his life or to hers. Besides, she'd probably be frightened or angry by the appearance of a strange man at her door claiming to be her late husband. This is only romantic in the movies! By daybreak, he had decided to send her a blessing and get on with his current life.

Later, back in Germany, he called a regression therapist he knew in Lindau. When the therapist heard the story, she agreed that Gerhard had done the right thing in leaving the widow alone. That lifetime was past for both of them. He had to remain dead to her.

Gerhard now feels that this past life explains his passionate interest in airplanes. Also, as a young boy growing up in Germany, he admired Wernher von Braun. He wanted to learn everything about the life of von Braun and devoured every bit of information he could find on him. He still has a scrapbook at home from this era with newspaper clippings and photos.

Gerhard used to live in Landshut, and Wernher von Braun had been brought to Landshut by the American military forces after the Second World War. He'd lived there for a short time until he was brought to America. Von Braun even got married in Landshut. Gerhard also got married in Landshut, even though neither he nor his wife lived there at the time or had any connection there. This is unusual in Germany; people usually get married where they live or in their local church.

The Executioner's Story

Another past life surfaced during this same vacation trip with Hermann. This occurred as they approached Wismar, a picturesque town in Germany by the East Sea.

As they drove into town, Gerhard had a most curious feeling that he knew this town well. Strong feelings of déjà vu stayed with him as they drove through the streets. Although he had never visited Wismar before in this lifetime, he pointed to a building in the distance and remarked to Hermann that it used to be a pharmacy. As they came nearer, they could see that it was indeed a pharmacy. A historical plaque on the building read that it had been a pharmacy since the sixteenth century.

They decided to go into a restaurant nearby for a bite to eat. This restaurant was a typical German guesthouse with long tables where the guests could mingle and sit together for their snacks and beer. There was an empty table on the terrace near the wall, and Gerhard took a seat while Hermann went off to find a restroom. Gerhard sat alone at the large table and looked around for someone to serve them. Although Gerhard tried to get his attention, the waiter passed the table several times without a glance in his direction. The room was crowded, and the table had room for twelve, but no one asked to join him at his big table. He sat alone, and the waiters continued to ignore him, serving others who had come in later. In the meantime, Gerhard was observing the other guests and passersby on the street. Suddenly, he noticed that his eyes were drawn to each person's neck. He was staring at every neck and imagining how the ropes would lie and where the noose must tighten! Even the necks of pretty young women seemed more fascinating to him at that moment than anything else.

When Hermann returned from the restroom, Gerhard was annoyed and nervous. He distinctly felt unwelcome and unwanted in this strange town, and he was disturbed by his thoughts of nooses and ropes and necks. He wanted to leave the restaurant immediately, and Hermann agreed.

Later, upon reflection and meditation, he was able to uncover some memories of a past life in this town, and he wanted to explore them at a deeper level. He asked Hermann to help him find an answer for this puzzle. He needed to find some explanation for his own behavior as well as his feeling of being someone that no one wanted to notice.

The regression revealed a past life, not surprisingly, as the public executioner or hangman for this community! Under hypnosis, he revealed that public executions were a great amusement in those days. People would walk in from the countryside, bringing their children and treating the entire affair like a carnival. Pickpockets were always present since a gathering of excited citizens was good for business! It was simply good theater.

The audience particularly liked it when the condemned person kicked and struggled against his fate. If he suffered more than was absolutely necessary, that was even better.

Gerhard said that sometimes he knew that the intended victim was innocent of the crime for which he was being punished. These few innocents had been placed in this terrible situation because of the greed of a local land baron who had designs on the condemned person's property. The law decreed that the condemned person's property was forfeit to the local authority—that being the land baron.

His job required that he perform executions, and he was trained to this end. When he was presented with an innocent victim, however, he looked for something he could do to ease their suffering. If the person was guilty of a crime, then he could just go about his business without any feelings of wrongdoing on his own part. Gerhard, as the hangman, had the professional know-how to insert a pin into the skull of the victim prior to tightening the rope, and this is what he sometimes did. In this way, the victim's suffering would be less, death would come much more quickly, and the mob would be deprived of their "show."

After this unsettling experience in Wismar, and in the pursuit of his healing ministry, Gerhard has now come into contact with and recognized three of these reincarnated souls. He found the hangman's noose in the auras and then felt the pins in their skulls. At the same time, he saw an image of what he had done so many hundreds of years before. The process of removing the ropes—and the pins— has released his own karmic injury as well as those of his clients.

Some weeks later, when he came back from Wismar, he received a call from an acquaintance named Connie. She asked if she could come over because she had problems with her thyroid and wanted to have a healing. This was not the first time that he had a done a healing for her, so he agreed and asked her to come right over.

As he began to feel her aura, he was surprised to see that she was holding her head low, almost like Princess Diana used to carry herself. This was not her usual posture, and Gerhard was struck by the different attitude. However, he began his healing procedure. As he felt her aura, he found a blockage on her throat. In the same moment, he got a picture of a hanged person. Still working in her aura, he pushed his hand against the throat area. She immediately had difficulty breathing. He pulled an imaginary rope in an upward stroke. She reacted violently, exclaiming, "Are you crazy? That hurts! I can't breathe! I can't get any air!"

Gerhard apologized. "Sorry, I just found a noose in your aura."

Gerhard knew that he found a past life pattern. He knew that his impression of a hanging was probably correct and that he had to remove the rope from her neck.

He asked her to turn her head from right to left and see if she could feel anything unusual. She did so and exclaimed, "There's still something at my neck! It feels like a pin, and it hurts a lot."

A pin! Gerhard placed his hands in the area where she pointed, and suddenly, to his surprise, he found what really felt like a pin! He knew instantly that he was the one who had placed this pin in the physical body of the woman who was hanged in that prior life. He removed it with a deep feeling of resolution and fulfillment. They had been connected down the ages with this single pin that he had inserted so many hundreds of years ago and that was now just a stored memory pattern. He removed the pin. She felt the pain release immediately.

However, at the moment he removed the pin, he saw an image of a pair of red shoes sitting unused and unworn upon a closet shelf in the woman's home.

He asked her, "Do you have some new red shoes in your closet that you can't bring yourself to wear in public?"

"Yes," she replied. "I bought them because I liked them, but every time I plan to wear them, I change my mind. I can't seem to wear them out of the house. How do you know that? Even my husband doesn't know about those shoes!"

Gerhard shrugged. He then received the impression that she had been a wealthy woman during the Middle Ages and had owned a pair of fine red leather shoes. Red leather was a real luxury and rarity at that time. It took a special dye to make leather shoes turn a red color, and that special dye was much too dear for most people to buy. She was the only one in town who owned red shoes!

A wealthy, elderly neighbor with an elegant house lived next door, and the woman had been taking care of her since she had no relatives. When the neighbor died, it turned out that she had left her property to the friend that had taken such good care of her. Unfortunately, a powerful baron, a member of the city council, coveted the house and schemed to get it for himself. He paid a witness to swear that he had seen a woman wearing a long cloak and red shoes go into the neighbor's house and kill her. Because of the false testimony and the fact that she was the only woman in the village to own a pair of red shoes, she was sentenced for this crime, and her property was forfeited to the baron's treasury.

This was one of the most profound events that Gerhard had ever experienced. He thought about how many times he had met Connie and her husband for coffee and the times she had been to his home for a healing. He thought of how often they had met on the street or market. There was not one thing to make either of them aware that they shared a past life connection.

He thought about the timing of this incident. The memory of the Wismar life was still in sharp focus in his consciousness, and now he had the victim of a hanging standing before him! No inkling had he ever received of a past life relationship with Connie! It was only the way she held her head at this particular meeting that made him think of a hangman's victim. He wondered if the recent experiences in Wismar had triggered a past life memory in his own consciousness that made it possible for Connie to receive a healing for her thyroid problem. In this instance, Gerhard and Connie waited for several hundred years before the executioner and his victim came face-to-face again for the purpose of healing that karmic wound.

When he found the second pin in another person, he wondered if he would find any more. In the case of the second pin, he received no information on the circumstances of the "crime" for which the person was hanged. And then he found a third, but again, he received no further information to be passed on to the victim. (The headaches must have been ferocious!)

Gerhard noticed that of the three hanging victims with the pins in their auras, not one had any anger, hatred, or emotion directed at him when they were told that he was the one who tightened the noose and placed the pin so long ago.

Gerhard doesn't believe there could be many more of these victims because it was a very small town and executions weren't so commonplace. However, as can be imagined, the experience of meeting these people again had a profound effect on him. There seems to be a karmic resolution in progress when he meets these victims again and restores balance to their auras. A very special use for a very special gift.

The Volga Song

About 1993 or 1994, encouraged by Hermann, Gerhard decided that he wanted to experience past life regression therapy with a professional. He traveled to Lindau, an island in Lake Constance. It was the first time that he could actually experience and relive a past life memory in regression hypnosis. He found that it was very easy for him, like switching on a radio to the right broadcast station, and he was actually reliving scenes from a past life. At first, he thought that it was just a curious thing and that it was entirely possible that memories of a past life could be merely guided fantasies.

However, during this therapy, he had a very strange past life experience. The therapy itself started on a Monday morning. On Monday and Tuesday, he felt that he had made a lot of progress in finding past lives and was gratified that he could now explain some blockages and curious events in his life that had previously puzzled him.

On Tuesday evening, feeling very satisfied at his progress and experiences, he decided to leave his hotel room and walk down to the lake. There, he discovered one of those grand old European hotels with a pleasant promenade. A string orchestra was playing, so he found a table and ordered ice cream and coffee. He felt happy and contented with his workshop experiences and life in general.

Then, the orchestra conductor announced that they would play the Volga Song from Franz Lehar's operetta *Der Tsarevich*. Suddenly, for no reason, a great depression fell over him. He didn't understand why he had suddenly had his spirits cast down so low. It was as if he'd been doused with a cold shower, and it was tinged with fear. Why did this song suddenly have the power to make him feel so bad? He'd heard this song many times before without this strange depression.

These feelings were so overwhelming and strange that he felt he couldn't stay there any longer. He quickly paid his bill and began walking back to his own hotel. On the way back, he kept wondering about these emotions. He had often heard this song and never had problems. Why did it happen now? He knew that the Volga Song was connected to Russia but couldn't find a link to himself in his present life. He found himself with the thought that it would be a terrible thing to be buried in a foreign country, on foreign soil.

The next day, when he began his therapy session, he related this experience to the therapist. She advised him to try to come closer to the feeling of being buried in a foreign country. He began by telling the therapist that he felt it must have happened in North Africa—could be in Tunisia or Morocco or Algeria. He had a feeling that he had previously lived in Paris with his parents, and his father was a general in the army. It seemed that when he was about nineteen or twenty years old, he had wanted to pursue his education.

His father, however, had a different plan for him. He insisted that it was a family tradition for the oldest son to make a career in the French Army before studying. So, he became a soldier and went to North Africa.

He then suddenly had the feeling that he was lying in the sand in the night and was immobilized in some way. He couldn't move. He also had the sure knowledge that when the sun arose the next morning, he would be dead. He would be executed as a deserter. He was filled with fear and dread of what awaited him the next morning. It was well known that the French Army always selected the worst marksmen for the execution command. This was done with the intention that deserters didn't deserve a quick or merciful death. An example had to be made for the other soldiers to discourage desertion.

When the first morning light came, he saw the execution commander and recognized Hermann, his best friend in this life. He saw that Hermann had selected the best shooters of the battalion, and Gerhard was immediately relieved to see them. At the critical moment, he saw only the fire from the gun barrels and fell. His last thoughts were of how relieved he felt to die quickly, mixed with sadness that his mother in Paris wouldn't know what had happened to him. He'd been very close to his mother in this lifetime, and he thought sadly that she would never know where he had died or what had happened to him.

He knew that his father would never tell her about his fate. He had written a letter to his father and asked to be forgiven for his shameful crime of desertion but had received a reply that his father had no son who was a deserter! Gerhard then saw a grave and knew that he was buried there. Curiously, at that moment, he felt very happy because he saw a vision with pictures of soldiers one hundred years later. They were lying in the sand, and their bodies were open and animals came and ate their organs. Gerhard had the strange thought that he felt lucky to be buried in a grave and not left out on the ground. At that point in the therapy session, he was able to release the experience. After the session, he again felt happy and satisfied.

That evening, he went into a church for an organ recital. It ended at 9:50 pm and he remembered that the music at the Strand Hotel started at 9:30. He decided to go back to the promenade and listen to this music before he returned to his hotel. Just as he arrived, he heard the conductor say, "And now, we have a special request to play the Volga Song as an encore from yesterday evening." Gerhard sat down, ordered ice cream and coffee, and listened with contentment to the music that he couldn't bear to hear the previous evening. He felt no more negative emotions and felt totally released.

In order to explain how the music of the Volga Song became a trigger for Gerhard's past life memory, the plot of *Der Zarewitsch* concerns the difficult relationship between Peter the Great and his son, Alexei. Alexei was commanded by his father to become a monk or enter the military, and he responded by running away. Upon his return to Russia, he was imprisoned and tortured, dying before he could be executed. In the operetta, Alexei runs away and has a love affair, but gives up his true love to return to Russia upon his father's death and succeed him as the Tsar of Russia. In real life and in the operetta, the relationship with the father was an important factor. This relationship was an important element in Gerhard's past life regression.

Since this memory surfaced, Gerhard has felt ever closer to Hermann as a friend. When he told Hermann about this regression, they both agreed that it was very easy to imagine and that it rang true for each of them. Gerhard has accumulated more experiences about past lives now. Sometimes when he is talking with Hermann, he will suddenly receive information or a feeling. Hermann, who is a regression hypnotist, will immediately make a past life regression session with him to discover even more about their shared histories.

A Curious Turn of Events: Gerhard Becomes The Patient

Eight years later, in southern Germany, Gerhard held a seminar for doctors and medical practitioners. The seminar began on Friday afternoon. During the introduction, Gerhard felt a sudden sharp pain in his right upper jaw. He felt it begin to swell. He was in such pain that he was afraid that he would not be able to continue to lead the group.

Among the participants was a lady named Anja, who had taken part in one of Gerhard's previous seminars. He was familiar with her and knew that she was a gifted psychic who was able to see auras. He asked her if she would be able to help him. He told her that he had pain in the jaw, and she responded immediately that she could see that the upper right jawbone was shattered. Using the techniques she had learned from Gerhard, she performed aura surgery and implanted a new jawbone.

She then inquired if he had problems with his neck.

He responded, "No, I have never had problems with my neck."

The pain was still there. The group took a break, and he went to his hotel room. Suddenly, he felt that he was bleeding, and when he went to the bathroom, he found that blood was actually flowing from the back of his mouth. In that moment, he noticed that the pain had disappeared. That was the end of that, and he was able to continue the seminar without further problems.

However, the next day, when he was guiding a meditation, he felt a sudden sharp pain in his neck. He called on Anja again and asked if she could help him. She reminded him very nicely that she told him the day before that he had a problem there. Now she could see there was a bullet lodged in his aura! Again, she operated on him, and he felt immediate relief from the pain.

The memory of that experience he had so many years ago regarding the Volga Song now came suddenly to mind. He knew that the bullet he now felt in his neck was the bullet from the execution as a result of his desertion on the battlefield in North Africa. He was finally healed of that karmic injury. It was curious as to how and when it had resurfaced. It was undoubtedly the presence of Anja, the healer, that had triggered it.

As a side note, Gerhard's upper right jawbone has always been thicker than the upper left jawbone. He had first been made aware of this by a dentist, who remarked that it was unusual. It was so interesting to the dentist that he made an impression for his collection. That was some years prior to the events in this seminar, of course.

This might be a good place to explain Gerhard's theories on the mechanics of aura injuries and healing. The aura is generally described to be composed of seven levels: 1. etheric, 2. emotional, 3. mental, 4. astral, 5. etheric template, 6. celestial, and 7. causal.

Gerhard feels the three most important levels which are related to his work are:

1. the etheric level, which is most closely connected to the material body and duplicates the material body, including all the organs, in every respect; 2. the emotional body, which contains memories from the present lifetime, as well as memories from prior lives; and 3. the spiritual level, which is the location of our higher selves. This higher self may not be very interested in the bullet, noose, or knife or circumstances of death in one lifetime but only in the workings of the relationships and soul growth.

It could be that the emotional part of the aura is still suffering. This energy is going to the material body and causing pain or other trauma because every living cell has a memory and a consciousness. This memory is not limited to the time and space in which it occurred. It is connected to the life force of the being who suffered the trauma.

However, if there is a blockage in the emotional body, the higher self may not be able to connect with the etheric level and heal the wounds that are manifesting on the material body. The higher self cannot be ill or diseased because it has a perfect blueprint or matrix.

8

Visiting the Philippines and Psychic Surgeons

Miracles do not happen contrary to nature; they
happen contrary to what we know of nature.
                                    —St. Augustine

GERHARD TURNED FIFTY IN 1996. He considered this a mile-
stone birthday, and he wanted to make a very special trip
as a birthday gift for himself. He had a lifelong dream to go
to Hawaii and thought about that as a birthday destination.
Whenever he saw pictures of Hawaii or heard Hawaiian
music, he was enthralled. He told some friends of his plan
to go to Hawaii, and they all agreed that it was too long a
trip from Germany for the limited time of his vacation.
One friend suggested that he go to Manila because of his
interest in psychic or spiritual healing. Why not go and see
how those famous psychic surgeons are working? They're
doing sensational things, and that should be very interesting.

That sounded like a good idea. He decided to stop off
in Hong Kong. It happened to be the last year before Hong

Kong was returned to China. He set off on his journey and had two wonderful days in Hong Kong before he arrived in Manila. Gerhard inquired immediately at his hotel how he could find the famous psychic surgeons. They advised him to go across the street to a certain marketplace and look for guides that were also taxi drivers. They could take him to the best psychic surgeons.

However, a funny thing happened when he found his two guides. They asked him if he were ill because he was looking for the psychic healers.

"No," Gerhard replied, "I'm not ill. I am a healer myself in Germany, and I want to see for myself what the healers here are doing."

The taxi drivers became very excited. One of them said, "Oh, if you are a healer, then you must see Mario's sister-in-law. She has something wrong with her legs, and she's been unable to walk for the last fourteen years."

Gerhard was a little surprised at this turn of events but agreed to see Mario's sister-in-law and try to heal her. They drove and drove and drove. Finally, he was brought to an area that can only be described as the slums. Gerhard termed this area a most cruel section of Manila, the worst and most miserable slums anyone could imagine. He admitted to feeling a little more than nervous. He had never seen such poverty or conditions. He'd never seen anything this bad in his entire life. No one knew where he was, either. Perhaps he had made a mistake to allow these men to bring him here. Perhaps he would never come out.

But they did finally arrive in front of a shack. He was escorted without fanfare into a dark room, where a woman was lying on a rough cot, much like an Army bed. She attempted to get up but couldn't come to her feet. With help, she was able to stand and take a few steps by holding onto a table, but then her knees buckled, and she collapsed.

She sat down in a straight wooden chair. Gerhard knelt

before her and asked for healing energy in his hands. He was guided then to lay his hands on her knees and massage energy into them.

She exclaimed, "Oh, I feel something going right down my legs to the ankles!"

The healing lasted a very short time, and he told her that she should feel better by tomorrow and perhaps would be able to walk. Gerhard promised he would return for another visit if she didn't feel better the next morning.

The driver then returned him to his hotel. They made arrangements for him to be driven on a sightseeing tour of Manila, including a trip to the famous psychic surgeons, the next day.

The next morning, the guides were waiting for him as he came down to the lobby of his hotel. Mario asked if he would make a return visit with them to the slums.

"Why?" asked Gerhard. "Is your sister-in-law worse?"

"No, she's walking. She's walking all over the neighborhood, and everyone has seen her walking around. Now all the neighbors say I should bring this healer back, and they are waiting to see you."

So, Gerhard returned to the slums. He went from house to house with his guides and healed the entire day. He returned every day for the next nine days. He healed for up to fourteen hours per day. He was on his feet the entire day, and he'd only had a little water and some fruit to eat. But he wasn't tired—on the contrary, at the end of each day, he felt a deep satisfaction and peace.

When it was time for him to leave Manila, he realized that he hadn't seen any part of the country except the shabby neighborhood where he had worked. He also hadn't seen any psychic surgeons! He estimates that he saw about eighty people in this short time period.

Today, when he speaks of this trip, he is still deeply impressed by what he was privileged to accomplish. The impressions of that trip were the impetus to continue in healing as a lifetime vocation. He promised the people that he would return in the autumn.

He did return in November 1996 for ten days and this time saw over two hundred people! Again, he worked all day, every day.

Gerhard has one very moving memory from this trip. He was brought to meet a gentleman who appeared to be in his early fifties. He was suffering from the end stages of liver cancer, and his stomach protruded. He was in great agony and was lying in bed. Gerhard was disheartened because he thought he could do very little at this stage. However, Gerhard asked for guidance and was only led to lay his hands on the man's stomach, which seemed to make him relax. His breathing became a bit easier, and Gerhard sent healing energy to him. He then looked into his eyes and was very moved to see that the man was looking back at him with gratitude shining through his dark brown eyes. Gerhard was deeply touched by the connection he was sharing with this man. He removed his hand and blessed him.

He received a letter from the man's family shortly after his return to Germany. They wanted to let him know that he had died two weeks after the healing but that he had suffered no more pain. He was able to cross over in peace. Gerhard was deeply moved and still remembers his brief connection to this man with awe and gratitude to the universe.

These trips to Manila were extremely important for Gerhard since it was the final proof that he had the ability to help others and relieve suffering. Since that time, he has devoted more and more of his free time to this calling.

Oh, yes, he's still dreaming of a trip to Hawaii and is confident that he will someday have the opportunity to meet with healing kahunas.

9

Meeting Stephen Turoff and Beginning Aura Surgery

Physicists started believing in God again a long time ago, but only doctors still believe in physicists.

—German physicist Thure von Üxküll

The astral body is a precise counterpart of the physical body, its organs, its parts, its centres, and its cells. In fact, the astral body is the pattern upon which the physical body is materialized. The astral body is composed of an etheric substance of a very high rate of vibration. In one sense it may be considered as a very subtle form of matter—in another as a semi-materialized form of force or energy. It is finer and more subtle that the rarest vapors or gases known to science. And, yet, it has a strong degree of tenacity and cohesiveness that enables it to resist attacks from the material side of nature—each organ, part, centre or cell, of the physical body has its astral pattern or basis. In fact, the physical body has been built up, in whole and in all of its parts, on the pattern and base of the astral body. Moreover, in case of impaired functioning of the physical organs or parts, and impaired activity of the physical body, its limbs, etc., if we can manage to arouse the activities of the astral body we may cause it to re-materialize or re-energize the physical body, and thus restore health and activity to it. If the liver, for instance, is not functioning properly, we proceed to start up the activities of the astral counterpart of that organ, to the end that the physical organ may be re-energized, and recreated in a measure. All true psychic healing work is performed on the astral plane, before it manifests on the physical.

—from *Clairvoyance and Occult Powers*
by Swami Panchaqdasi Yogi
Publication Society, 1916.

GERHARD IS A GREAT Anglophile and travels to Great Britain frequently on holiday trips. In the course of his travels and workshops, he made the acquaintance of John Graham, a spiritualist medium working in London, and they became close friends. John talked a great deal about Stephen Turoff, a London healer and world-famous psychic surgeon. Gerhard learned that Stephen did psychic surgery with instruments and that he was quite well known in healing circles. Grant Solomon's book, *Stephen Turoff – Psychic Surgeon: The Story of an Extraordinary Healer*, was published in 1998 and revised in 1999. Turoff is a 224-pound, six-and-a-half-foot tall, middle-aged, Jewish-Christian former carpenter from Brick Lane in London's East End who many believe to be an instrument of God. Gerhard knew that he wanted to meet this healer.

John suggested that Gerhard get in touch with a German lady he knew, who was acquainted with Stephen and could introduce them. Gerhard was surprised to find that she lived in Landau, which was practically neighboring Landshut, where he lived. How surprising to find a local connection to the famous healer he longed to meet! Gerhard got her telephone number from John and called her. When he mentioned that he was a friend of John Graham's, she was astonished to find someone else in the neighborhood who shared her interest in spiritual healing and English mediums!

When she casually mentioned that she planned to make a journey to visit Stephen Turoff in April 1997, Gerhard jumped at the chance to accompany her group. There were about eighteen or twenty of them, and he met his traveling companions for the first time at the airport in Munich. Gerhard felt very comfortable and compatible with them right away. They were off to visit the famous healer! The Hotel Miami was in Chelmsford, and it was right next door to Stephen's Danbury Healing Clinic.

Gerhard made an appointment to see Stephen. The clinic consisted of a waiting room and two rooms where the healer consulted with his patients. When it was Gerhard's turn, he wrote the purpose of his visit on a card and was instructed to lie down on a recliner. Stephen's healing technique consisted of working in the aura with surgical instruments. During the course of his treatment, Stephen casually asked him what he did in Germany. Gerhard told him his occupation but added that he was very interested in what Stephen was doing. He asked if it were possible to learn this kind of spiritual healing.

Up until that time, Gerhard had only worked with his hands to feel the aura and find disturbances and past life patterns. Stephen performed surgery with instruments and worked closely with spirit guides, the guides presumably being physicians from the other side who had agreed to work with him.

Stephen said that the kind of healing he performed wasn't possible to learn because he worked with and received assistance from his personal spirit guide, Dr. Kahn. Dr. Kahn had supposedly lived in Austria, where he died in 1912. Stephen encouraged Gerhard to try to find his own guidance. He had only to ask for a spirit doctor, and perhaps one would agree to appear and work with him.

At the end of his healing session, Gerhard came out of the healer's room to find that the rest of his group had already gone back to their hotel rooms. However, he was excited and energized by what he had seen and experienced, so he set out for a walk. He just wanted to walk and think. He believes that he walked for an hour and a half, starting very briskly and then walking more and more slowly as he thought about everything that he had seen and experienced.

When he finally returned to the hotel, he found the others, and they discussed their individual experiences over dinner. The next day, he had another treatment scheduled with Stephen and again expressed his interest in spiritual healing and his desire to emulate Stephen's healing technique. Gerhard persisted, "How can I learn to do what you're doing?"

Stephen responded, "Let's try it and see what happens. Go back to your hotel room and wait to see if I can send a patient to you."

Gerhard went to his room and waited. He didn't have to wait very long at all.

A knock on the door signaled the arrival of his first patient. A woman was standing at the door. She said, "Stephen said I should come to you because I have problems with my gallbladder."

She explained that her gallbladder had been surgically

removed and that the incision had been closed with clamps and not with stitches.

"They removed the clamps," she explained, "but since then, I've had the feeling that the clamps were still there. I feel them! The doctors insist that all the clamps were removed and that it's impossible for me to feel something that isn't there, but I do!"

Gerhard had nothing with him except a laser pointer, pincers, and a pair of small scissors. He pulled with his pincers in the area where the incision for the gallbladder might have been made and asked if she could feel something.

"No, nothing there."

He moved a little bit and pulled again. "Can you feel that?"

"Yes."

"And this?"

"Yes."

"And this?"

"Yes."

He found six clamps in all and removed them. He simply cut them off with his scissors. When she left, she was pain free and felt that all the clamps had been left behind with Gerhard.

Almost immediately, a young man arrived and said that Stephen told him that he should check his spine. Gerhard did surgery on the spine and then asked him to try to move. He also reported no more pain and left feeling much better.

Then, someone came with stomach problems, and he worked with him.

And so it went for the rest of the day. Every case was different, and Gerhard seemed to know what to do. After this experience, the people in Gerhard's group heard about what he was doing, and they also came to him for healing. Gerhard found it amusing that these friends had traveled all the way to London and ended up with him for a healer! He found more and more confidence in what he was doing with every healing that he performed.

Experiences in Aura Surgery

Back home in Germany, the people in the group he had traveled with to meet Stephen Turoff were talking to their friends and families about Gerhard and what they'd seen him do in London. Gerhard got a call one day from a local woman named Renate, who had heard about him from someone in this group. She lived nearby and told Gerhard that her son's fiancée was suffering from breast cancer and there was no hope for her recovery. Renate asked him if he could do something for her. Gerhard responded that he really didn't know. This was the first time that he'd been asked to heal a seriously ill person, but he agreed to come and try.

He was brought to the bedroom of a very young lady, about twenty-four or twenty-five. Gerhard asked her if she could stand up so that he could check her aura. It was then that he found his first earthbound soul in the aura. In the process of the examination, his spirit guides told him that he didn't have to do surgery this time. He was guided to give three injections in the liver, but he had no syringes with him. So, he simply imagined a syringe and made the prescribed injections in the liver area. Then he received guidance that he could do nothing else but wait.

Later, Renate told him that the young lady got up after he left, took a bath, and spent the entire day without any pain. Three days later, she fell into a coma, and three days after that, she died. The young lady's doctor was told about the spiritual healer who had visited. The doctor was receptive to the idea and remarked that in this case, it was a very fortunate thing that she had died so quickly—that normally, she would have suffered a very long time with a great deal of pain. If she had not died, she would have had a cruel and unending headache and would probably have become like a baby. She would have been crying the entire day.

Since then, Gerhard resolved to buy needles, syringes, and instruments to facilitate his surgeries. Some people have remarked on whether or not these are really necessary, but he feels they help to focus his thoughts and concentrate his energies. It could be that the instruments and their use help to focus healing energy from the patient's standpoint also. It's possible that the sight of the instruments may send healing pictures to the higher self.

Surgery for Hermann the Warrior

Sometime later, during one of Gerhard's continuing workshops, he had eaten breakfast in the hotel with his friend Hermann. After breakfast, Hermann asked Gerhard if he would feel his aura. He said that he had a lot of pain in his jaw. When Gerhard felt Hermann's aura, he felt something metallic in the jaw area. He had his laser pointer with him because he'd been using it to highlight points with a projector during his workshop.

Gerhard used the pointer to open Hermann's aura. There, he found a special kind of metal that he couldn't identify.

After he removed it, Hermann said, "I have a taste in my mouth like metal." But the pain in his jaw was gone.

Hermann is a very special case for Gerhard, and the most impressive spiritual healing he'd performed at this time involved him. One day, soon after the metallic pieces had been removed from Hermann's aura, they were sitting side by side on the sofa in Hermann's living room. Gerhard suddenly felt there was something different, that something wasn't quite right with Hermann. He pointed to the middle of Hermann's forehead and asked him if he had pain there.

"Yes, I do," he said.

"Can you feel this?" Gerhard asked, moving his hand in the area.

"Yes, I can feel it—it hurts!"

"And here too?" Gerhard persisted.

"Yes, that hurts too."

Gerhard told him that it felt like an arrow in his aura.

Hermann said, "Well, go ahead and take it out, then." So he pulled it out, and Hermann said that he felt better. Then Hermann said, "Look in my ear; I feel the same pain there."

Gerhard found another arrow and pulled it out. Then, he pulled something from the right ear. Gerhard laughs today when he tells how many spears and arrows he pulled from Hermann's body that day. Hermann was truly a warrior in many prior lifetimes.

The next morning at breakfast, Renate, Hermann's wife, said that something curious had happened. "Hermann always coughs a lot every morning when he gets up, but not today."

Since that time, Hermann has had no more of these headaches and doesn't cough in the morning.

This was one of the many experiences that first led Gerhard to accept the reality of reincarnation and the effect of past lives and injuries. Hermann believed in reincarnation and performed past life hypnosis and regression experiments. These regressions revealed that Hermann had been a soldier in many lives and had picked up the spears and arrows in North Africa, France, and England, especially during the Middle Ages.

Hermann was the first person in whose body he found and removed arrows. He was also the first person on whom Gerhard performed aura surgery for past life karmic injuries! Up until that time, he treated symptoms successfully but didn't give a great deal of thought as to karma and past life experiences.

A Tonsillectomy

Another curious healing took place with a woman from Landau. She came to Gerhard with a sore throat, and he found that her tonsils were causing the problem. After her aura surgery, she felt much better. Gerhard reports that he removed the tonsils in the aura. He did this, of course, without actually touching the throat or mouth of his client.

The woman contacted him some time later after a routine visit to her doctor revealed that the tonsils were gone! She said, "The doctor asked me what happened to my tonsils, and I told him that I'd been to a healer."

The doctor didn't believe her and asked where the operation had taken place.

Still in Shock—Fatal Injuries

Gerhard works frequently in the offices of naturopaths and helps them in difficult cases where the normal treatments seem ineffective. During one of these cases in February 2003 in the German town of Forchtenberg, a man arrived for routine treatment for an arthritic knee. As is normal for treating knee problems, the man was seated in a chair, and Gerhard in another chair, facing him.

Gerhard began his treatment and found the problem in the left knee. He began by opening the aura with one of his surgical knives. He then did a cleansing of the area and finally injected new joint lubrication in the knee. Finally, in order to complete and support the treatment, Gerhard laid his hand upon the man's knee to massage the injected fluid into the joint. Up to that point, no physical contact whatsoever had been made with the knee.

Without pausing to look up at his patient, Gerhard then asked him to move his leg. There was no response. He repeated his request, but there was still no answer or movement from the man. Gerhard then looked up at his patient and saw that he seemed to be in a state of deep shock. Beads of perspiration had appeared on his forehead, and his lips were totally without color. The patient's wife, who was sitting nearby, was able to see auras. With excitement, she told Gerhard that the aura surrounding the lower half of the man's leg had suddenly disappeared and she couldn't see anything there at all. At the same moment, Gerhard received information from his spiritual guide, a doctor, that the man's leg had been ripped off at the knee in a prior lifetime! At that moment, he was reliving the shock that he had suffered in that prior lifetime.

Gerhard quickly pulled the energy back into the leg and found the arteries and veins he needed to reconnect in the aura to restore circulation in the lower leg. Then, he used a needle and thread to reconnect the bonds of this etheric knee back into the aura. He closed the aura again with these stitches.

He then received guidance to give an injection of medicine directly into the aura by the heart and another injection into an arm vein. It was only then that the man recovered his ability to speak. He related that he could hear Gerhard's voice and that of his wife as if from a great distance, but he couldn't move a muscle during that time.

Gerhard noted that this wasn't the first time that a patient had such a reaction to a harmless and ordinary aura healing. Gerhard had come into contact with an old injury and shock that hadn't been totally released in the aura.

Later, in speaking of this incident with the doctor, he made an observation that these old wounds could be the reason that some people have such violent reactions to a routine and harmless treatment in a doctor's office or emergency room. Some patients have even suddenly died for no discernible reason.

The explanation is that the surgeon or doctor may be operating on a patient that had suffered from a shock or injury in another life. If the doctor chances to contact that part of the aura where this information is stored, the memory may be released with all the attendant shock. The patient will suffer the full shock of that prior injury, and the doctor will have no idea what has happened, let alone how to effectively reverse the shock. If the doctors don't believe in unresolved past life patterns, then they have no effective tools to treat them. The wounds will go untreated and unhealed.

Gerhard encountered a similar experience just a few weeks later when he was examining the aura of a young woman. He found needles in the aura left over from a previous life. As he removed one of his injection needles from the aura of her right arm, she said that she suddenly felt dizzy, and then she lost consciousness.

Gerhard quickly administered an injection into her aura and laid his hands on her solar plexus. She regained consciousness then and related to Gerhard how she had always feared injections and needles and suffered panic attacks at the sight of needles since childhood. In this lifetime, she had never been hospitalized for any reason or suffered from any illness or condition requiring frequent injections. In other words, there was no trauma in this lifetime that could lead to an overwhelming fear or panic of injections and needles.

Gerhard had found a needle in the aura that was still in the veins. He wondered if it was the remaining energy pattern of a lethal injection from a prior life, where she died with the needle embedded in the vein. Since Gerhard removed that pattern, she has recovered from these panic attacks and can face an injection without incurring one.

Chains on an Amputated Leg

In April 2003, Gerhard found himself again in the doctor's office in Forchtenberg, where an elderly lady in a wheelchair was brought to him for treatment. The woman had lost both legs to diabetes, the right leg from above the knee and the left leg just below the knee. Gerhard found the patterns of slavery in her aura, consisting of a yoke over the shoulders. As he removed this yoke, she said that her shoulders and upper body immediately felt much lighter. It was Gerhard's experience that if the yoke was present around the shoulders and neck, there were bound to be chains around the ankles. So he set about to remove the chains from her feet. His normal procedure is to find the chains in the aura around the ankles and then ask the patient to move the feet to check if they are lighter. Since she had no feet, he asked her to raise her thighs from the wheelchair. He then tried to find the energy patterns of the feet and removed the etheric chains. After this happened, the woman was laughing as she moved her thighs up and down in the wheelchair. She said that her legs had never felt so light.

This means that even when the arms and legs have been amputated, the energy patterns remain with any wounds and injuries. Without a doubt, many complaints of a patient that cannot be treated by conventional scientific wisdom can be traced to old injuries to the etheric body that have not been spiritually healed.

Ideally, physicians could be trained to spot karmic patterns and refer patients to a practitioner that can counsel and treat them at the proper karmic level. The consequences of the karmic past can sometimes be found in the aura. They definitely have an effect on the health and well-being of an individual in the present life. This is the reason why ordinary physicians cannot always effect a cure - they can only treat issues which affect the physical body. If the injury or pattern is in the aura, it is not obvious to a physician, of course. A drowning in a past life, for example, might cause a person to suffer lung problems, asthma, or other lung related illnesses. A spider bite or snakebite releases toxins into the energy field which can cause a great deal of nerve damage in future lifetimes. Ordinary medical care will not erase the energy pattern in the aura and can only offer temporary relief of the pain or discomfort. The patient can only be healed when the problem is treated at its source. A regular physician can determine if the health issue is related to an actual physical condition which can be treated at the physical level. If no organic cause can be discovered, the physician should consider the possibility of karmic damage in the aura.

Healing a Concert Pianist

Gerhard was contacted by a medical doctor that had a patient who had developed a problem with his fingers on the right hand. Since the patient was a concert pianist, this problem had already affected his professional abilities, and he was in a very bad situation. He had lost most of the feeling in the tips of his fingers. He entered a research hospital for tests to determine the reason for the disability. After numerous tests had been conducted by the doctors and scientists, they did confirm that he had nerve damage that drastically reduced sensation in the nerve endings of the fingers on his right hand, but they confessed they had no treatment or prescription that would be effective. Since conventional medicine had offered no relief, his friends encouraged him to seek treatment with alternative medicine. Thus it was that he found a holistic physician who examined him and thought this might be a case for

Gerhard. He had worked with Gerhard before and had good results with the cases he had referred to him.

Gerhard met with the patient in the doctor's office. After feeling the aura, Gerhard found nothing relating to past life injuries. But he immediately knew that he must perform aura surgery on the right shoulder and that it would be successful. And it was. Two weeks later, the pianist was able to resume his career. He told his doctor that during the healing, he felt that all the sensation had returned. He made a point of revisiting the famous research facility to meet with the doctor that could not help him before. More tests were performed, and they could find nothing wrong. He asked the doctors if they wanted to know how he had been helped. They were eager to learn until they found that he was healed by aura surgery! At that point, they threw their hands up and almost threw him out of their offices. Conventional medicine has no understanding for this kind of treatment, which is not being taught in medical schools.

However, Europeans are much more open to alternative healing because of their long reliance on heilpraktikers (healing practitioners). Heilpraktikers are recognized in Germany and must have a degree in naturopathy in order to open an office and see patients. They are educated on medical issues and health care, but specialize in alternative treatments, such as homeopathy, Ayurvedic medicine, acupuncture, reflexology, and so forth.

Many patients are referred to Gerhard by these healing practitioners when these methods fail to heal them. It is not unusual for Gerhard to visit a practitioner's office on a weekend and see patients who have not responded to previous treatments. Frequently these patients have seen conventional physicians before they consulted the healing practitioner. Gerhard has great successes with these patients because the orthodox treatments have already failed, signaling the higher probability of the problem being karmic in nature.

It is important to remember that not every illness or injury can be healed! Some karmic patterns have been chosen by the individual before the earth plane has been entered. It can be explained as a desire to create an experience in this lifetime which will enhance spiritual growth and learning. Tht may involve struggling with an illness or physical handicap. Even though the individual may consciously yearn for a healing, the higher self may not give permission.

The Inexplicable Healing of Josefine S.

In late April 2001, Josephine S. telephoned Gerhard from her hospital room and asked for an appointment. She had heard about this aura surgeon and hoped she could get a reading immediately. She had just been diagnosed with type 2 diabetes and was depressed because it was the latest in a series of misfortunes. Two years before, she had undergone surgery to have her left ovary removed and then had been involved in an accident where a heavy-duty truck had rolled over her foot. She had been taken to the emergency room, where she was treated for the injury and given pain medication. No one had checked her blood then, and she thought about how her diabetic condition could have been discovered earlier. She had now been on medication for several months, but it wasn't enough to keep her blood sugar under control. It had been steadily climbing, and now it was at 407!

Her doctor had recommended daily insulin injections, but she was reluctant to give in to the diagnosis. In a last hope measure, she telephoned the healer her friend had told her about. Amazingly, even though it was a weekend,

Gerhard invited her to come straight away to the office of a general practitioner who worked regularly with him.

Even though she was a patient in a hospital, she got dressed and went to the address she was given. Her next appointment with her doctor was Monday morning, and he expected to run new tests and begin insulin injections. She was desperate for anything. She hoped that he might at least enable her to remain with her medication and not begin with the injections.

She was a little shocked when she saw all his surgical instruments lined up so neatly on a table in the office, which brought back memories of her surgery and the accident. She expected spirituality, not stainless steel scissors and knives! Gerhard was standing with his back to her and was busily replacing plastic intestines in a model of the human body that had removable parts. How curious was this?

Gerhard turned to her and asked, "Did you come directly from the hospital?"

She was reassured by his friendly smile and open manner. "Direct," she replied. She had received permission from the hospital to leave but hadn't told them where she was going. She needed to return immediately after the treatment.

He asked her to stand up so that he could scan her aura. She did, and he raised both hands until they were over her head. He then closed his eyes and let the hands slowly and gently come down around her. At the level of her neck, his hands stopped. He asked, "Do you have problems with your throat, hoarseness, muscle tension, or something similar?"

She answered, "Yes, I do."

He nodded and then moved his hand up and down directly in front of her throat. Then he pulled his hands down and back to the throat. "Do you feel pressure now?"

"Yes," she responded.

He nodded, and then reached behind her and clasped

something invisible and suddenly pulled up sharply, as if it were a rope.

"Did you feel something?" he asked.

"Yes, I can't breathe."

Gerhard smiled happily because he had found the problem. He went back to his table and found a pair of scissors and returned to her. He grasped the etheric rope into his hands and used the scissors to cut the noose free.

"Is this better?"

Josefine could scarcely believe it. "Yes, it is better— much better, as a matter of fact."

How did this work? What had he done? Before she could ask the questions, Gerhard explained, "It's possible that you were hanged in a previous life."

He made it seem to be the most natural explanation in the world. He then told her to try to turn her head to the left and to the right. She did and was surprised that she could indeed turn her head better than she had been able to for a long time. Josefine was delighted at how much easier it was, but Gerhard wasn't. He frowned and went back to his table. He returned with a spatula. He asked her to turn around so that he could get her neck into the right position to operate.

Even though she wanted to see what he was doing she obeyed and turned her back to him. She thought it was probably better that she didn't see what he planned to do with the spatula. She could feel him gently moving behind her and his hands moving at her neck, but he never touched her physically.

At last, he asked her to turn her head to the left and to the right again. She hadn't felt a thing while he was moving his hands up and down in the air around her neck. She was surprised that she was able to turn her head freely and completely to the left side without the usual little crick—and no pain whatsoever. She was overwhelmed that the little pain was completely gone. She could move her head freely now. Gerhard told her that the pain was gone and the memory of the rope had been removed. He asked her to stand again and raised his hands over her head and continued with his testing of the aura.

This time, his hands stopped at the level of her pelvic area. He asked if she needed to use the bathroom frequently, especially at night. She replied that wasn't the case with her unless she had drunk too much in the evening prior to going to sleep.

He asked, "Do you still have your appendix?"

"Yes, it's still there," she replied.

"How about other organs?" he persisted. "Are they all still there?"

"Everything," she responded, forgetting her missing left ovary for the moment.

"Funny," mused Gerhard, "I feel something is missing, as if there's a hole of some kind."

Josefine suddenly remembered the left ovary. It seemed impossible that he could feel that it was missing, but he had. She told him about the missing ovary and added that sometimes she felt a slight twitch or pain in that area. Without another word, he turned back to his instruments and found a pair of tweezers and a surgical needle. He told Josefine that he would operate in the energy field to close the opening. He worked with his instruments in the aura and explained that he was mending the opening with stitches. Shortly, he announced that he was finished and that the operation was successful.

Josefine felt a bit disappointed. She hadn't felt anything while he was sewing. She then explained her medical history to Gerhard, including the diabetes diagnosis and her last six weeks in the hospital with the ongoing blood sugar problems.

Gerhard listened carefully and then felt cautiously in the area of her stomach and solar plexus, inquiring where she felt pain, and noticed that she responded when he made movements over her solar plexus.

"Yes, I may see the problem," he said. He got up and left the room for a moment. He returned with a woman, who introduced herself as a reflexology therapist. She asked Josefine to seat herself, and the therapist pulled up a chair and seated herself. She asked for Josefine's foot.

Gerhard explained, "I believe I know the problem and have asked her to check upon a specific organ to confirm my suspicion."

The therapist nodded and examined the area of the foot he requested.

"Yes, here it is—does it hurt you here?" she asked, touching a place on her foot.

"Ow! Oh, yes," cried Josephine and drew her foot away quickly.

Gerhard seemed pleased and went back to his instruments. He came back with a hypodermic syringe. As he opened the package and pulled out the needle, he reassured Josefine that she would feel no pain at all from the symbolic injection. He explained that he thought there was a blockage at the intersection between the pancreas and the gallbladder, making it impossible for the insulin to reach the intestinal area.

Josefine asked Gerhard if the blockage might have resulted from too much pus in the abdomen two years ago. He responded that he didn't know if that was the reason but he would make the insulin flow again. He closed his eyes and held the syringe before his forehead. He gently pulled on the plunger until he seemed satisfied, and then placed the syringe into the abdominal area and guided the needle with a rotary motion into her aura. He gave an injection, paused for a moment, and moved the syringe at different angles, turning it as he moved, as if he were drawing something out of the area.

Josefine felt that something had been pulled out of her and asked him what had happened. He explained that he had rinsed the area and then pulled out the blockage. He moved his hand over her solar plexus and asked, "Do you feel anything now? Do you have any pain?"

She replied, "No, no pain now."

Gerhard asked the reflexologist to test Josefine's foot again. This time, there was no reaction at all.

Josefine left the office in wonder. She felt that she had actually been healed. She had no doubt whatsoever.

Josefine returned to the hospital and went directly into the shower. When she came out, she told her roommate everything that had happened to her that afternoon. As she pulled on her robe, her roommate pointed to a small, fresh nick just below the solar plexus.

She asked, "Did the aura surgeon prick you with a needle?"

"No, of course not. He never touched my skin—how could that be?"

Josefine was filled with pleasure at this tiny proof of her surgery. To her, this was an unmistakable sign that she had been healed.

On the following Monday, April 23, 2001, her doctor examined her and drew blood for the final results before beginning the planned insulin injections. When he reviewed the new blood tests, he was astonished to see that her blood sugar levels were completely normal. He asked the lab to check the reports, thinking there had been a mix-up in the results. The tests were repeated twice more, and no error was found. Finally, he announced that everything now appeared completely normal with this patient. Her blood sugar count was perfectly fine, and no treatment or diet change of any kind was needed.

The physicians finally came to the conclusion that she was free of diabetes, but they warned her that it would probably return sooner or later because their earlier tests could not be mistaken. Her blood sugar remained stable, and by the end of May 2001, she still had no diabetic symptoms. As of her last report in 2012, she has still never used insulin.

Several months after the operation, Josefine noticed that she hadn't felt any sudden pains from her left groin anymore. Her miraculous healing of diabetes made her wonder if Gerhard's sewing of the opening might also have led to a healing. She decided to go to a gynecologist that hadn't treated her before to have a full examination. The examination was routine, and the doctor reassured her that everything was in order.

She asked him to check again to see if anything was wrong, and new tests were run at her request. Again, nothing unusual turned up. Finally, she asked the doctor if anything was missing. Nothing, was the response. Everything was in order.

This was too much for her to believe. She asked the doctor point-blank if her left ovary was there.

The doctor laughed and said, "Of course. Why wouldn't it be there? It's there, and it's healthy."

She was shown the test results. Now the doctor wanted to know why she had so many questions about the left ovary, which was clearly in place and seemingly healthy.

She left the office without explaining the reason for her questions. She almost couldn't believe it herself. It was enough for her to know that she had been healed of diabetes and had regrown her left ovary as a bonus. She had certainly not expected that.

Josefine S. is still living today, over ten years after her appointment with Gerhard Kluegl, happy and healthy, with two ovaries and perfect blood sugar values. She is happy to tell everyone that he was her last hope and he worked a double miracle.

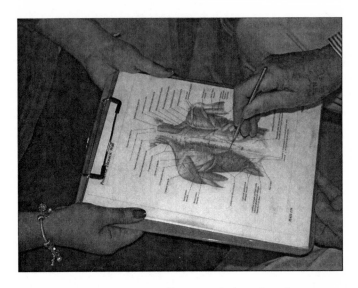

Fig. 1 Above. Using a needle on a clipboard with an anatomical illustration, Gerhard releases tension in the back muscles. The picture provides a focal point for the healer and patient.

Fig. 2 Below. At other times, Gerhard may use an anatomical model. In this illustration, he tests the sensitivity of the cardiac opening from the esophagus into the stomach.

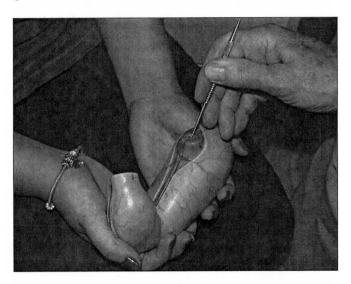

10

Organ Transplant with Aura Surgery

The person who wants to know and describe a
living thing will seek first to drive out the spirit,
then he has all the parts in his hand, but the spirit
holding it together is gone.

—J. W. Von Goethe

DR. X, A MEDICAL doctor in northern Germany, invited
Gerhard to come to his office in order to perform aura
surgery for one of his patients. The woman was about sixty
years old and suffered from kidney disease. The left kidney
had been removed. The remaining kidney was still working,
but at a very reduced level. A kidney specialist had advised
her that she needed dialysis. Before beginning dialysis,
however, she wanted to explore an alternative treatment.
So she visited a holistic doctor, and he used a dowsing rod to
determine if her consciousness would agree to this type of
treatment. The response was positive, and this doctor contacted Gerhard. At that point, Dr. X telephoned Gerhard

and invited him to meet her and see what could be done. He agreed to try to help her and made arrangements to travel to the doctor's office.

Gerhard attempted a new technique on this patient. He had acquired a plastic anatomical model that had removable parts. He removed the colon, stomach, and liver in order to get them out of the way so that he could see and touch the kidneys. She was lying on a massage table, and Gerhard asked her to hold the model with both hands against her body.

With a small, pointed instrument, Gerhard pressed against the model's right kidney, and she was able to feel the pressure in her own body. This is the indication that Gerhard has the necessary link to her physical body and, more important, the permission of her higher self to continue. Working together and using surgical instruments on the model, and with the cooperation of the medical doctor, they performed a virtual operation on the model, using the same procedures as a normal surgery.

Before he began the operation, Gerhard asked his spiritual advisors if it would be possible for him to receive a new kidney. He held a small plastic bowl in front of his third eye and received the necessary confirmation that the new organ had been placed into the bowl by his helpers on the other side. It is important for the reader to know that Gerhard is in charge of this consultation but that spiritual assistance is essential for success. By confirmation, Gerhard states that he just has a knowing feeling. He just knows that something is right or that something is not right.

The operation began in earnest. The kidney was virtually removed from the model with stainless steel surgical instruments and released or discarded into the universe. The new spiritual kidney was then placed into the model and connected to the correct arteries and veins and the urethra. No step was omitted from the surgery. Virtual connections were made to the arteries, veins, and urethra. He then closed the incision and blessed the operation and the patient. During this operation, the woman was holding the model at all times. She reported feeling that something was happening in the kidney area but wasn't uncomfortable and felt no pain. This was the first time that Gerhard or the holistic doctor had attempted this type of healing procedure.

Some days later, the doctor telephoned Gerhard to let him know that the new kidney was operating perfectly. The doctor that had recommended dialysis tested her and found that dialysis would not be necessary after all. Since that time, Gerhard has not heard from this doctor and can only believe that things are still well and good for the patient.

Organ Transplants and Energy

Gerhard has some thoughts and theories on the ethics and spiritual consequences of transplant surgery. These thoughts are based solely on his personal experiences and feelings and cannot be considered as imparted knowledge from the other side. He has no inside information on this subject. Because of the nature of his work, however, he has formed some conclusions and beliefs which may change as he matures and grows in his education. The following ideas are just that—ideas.

If an organ becomes diseased or injured for whatever reason and is replaced with another organ from a donor, one wonders if that "new" organ comes to the recipient with the "imprinted memory" of the donor. Does that imply that the recipient will suffer the effects of some unknown imprinting? What about the donor? If the donor was a young auto accident victim and his physical remains have been dissected and disseminated, would that create consequences for the donor in his next life or lives? Could he, for example, be born severely handicapped? Or does it depend on his belief system and his spiritual ability to deal with the consequences of the accident? There are a lot of questions.

Because each cell of your body is filled with your own consciousness, when a transplant operation is carried out, the consciousness part may feel that it is in a strange body. This may be one reason why the organ is not accepted by the recipient. If an organ is removed from a so-called dead body when the body is only clinically dead (i.e., the blood is still circulating, whether naturally or artificially), the consciousness may still be linked with the body. To this date, no one can, with any degree of scientific accuracy, prove when consciousness leaves the physical body. The nature of organ transplants, however, requires that the organ be fresh. For this reason, surgeons inject ice water into the body. If the donor still has a consciousness, this will impose a great stress, which may be experienced in every cell of the body.

In some hospitals, the doctors give anesthesia to the clinically living donor to prevent stress to the cells. Gerhard consulted a heart physician and asked him if this was a routine practice. He confirmed that some physicians recognized the need for anesthesia but did not know if every doctor did it routinely.

Some doctors had noticed that there was a physical reaction in the so-called dead patient when the first cut was made. Facial grimaces and muscular responses were observed. There can be serious psychological problems for the operating team when they record the stress reaction in a corpse.

The operating teams suffer emotional stress when they cause a patient to feel pain. How can anyone be positive that internal organs can be removed without pain before actual death occurs?

Anesthesia is always administered for the well-being of the recipient but is not always given for the comfort or alleviation of pain in the donor. A body will naturally react to the stress of surgery and organ removal by release of an enzyme-like substance, which will damage the organ and perhaps render it unfit for transplant. At any rate, the new organ will be at a different energy level than that of the body receiving the transplanted organ.

The general feeling among medical professionals is that there is no pain to the organ donor, but this cannot be proved in any way. Gerhard has spoken to a few operating room nurses who have told him that there is no emotional stress for operating room personnel that are performing an organ transplant on the recipient. On the other hand, medical personnel who are involved in removing the organ from the donor suffer much more emotional stress. This is natural since they are involved in the death of a human being

An article in the February, 2000 issue of *Anaesthesia*, Vol.33, Issue 3, pp.105-106, reported that even with administration of neuromuscular blocking agents, hypertension and tachycardia of the donor can be distressing for operating room personnel to witness. Although pain killers or sedation were not generally required for surgery on the organ donor, it should be administered, if only to reduce stress on the operating room personnel.

Another interesting point from Gerhard's view is whether or not the organ being transplanted is in resonance or agreement with the body into which it is being implanted. Could it be that the organ being transplanted does not agree with being placed into a new body? This might be proved by the fact that drugs must be administered for the rest of the recipient's life in order not to reject the organ.

This is an extremely complex issue, and not just from a clinical or physiological standpoint. The issues as Gerhard sees it are (1) consciousness, (2) agreement, and (3) all parties involved are at the appropriate level of spiritual engagement, including the donor, recipient, families, doctors, and nurses.

It may involve cruel and unrelieved pain for the donor. He is undoubtedly terminal; he will certainly die, but does he need to die in pain? How do we know what he or she is experiencing? There are so many books and stories written about near-death experiences and so-called trips to the other side that we are left to wonder as to when life actually ends.

Things may be changing, however. Anesthesia is now given routinely to brain-dead organ donors in a few countries because of these physiological reactions in the donor. It is Gerhard's hope someday that the atmosphere in the operating room become one of reverence for the gift. Ideally, the organ being removed should be blessed and a prayer offered that the organ can safely and successfully be separated from the energy of the donor, and then blessed again that it can be safely and successfully placed in the new body, reducing the risk of rejection and failure. In order to accomplish this, all the personnel on both operating teams should understand the nature of this event on both a physiological level and a spiritual level. A simple prayer would invoke a unity of purpose, and possibly make a difference between a successful transplant and a failed one.

We now know that each and every cell of our bodies is forever connected to our consciousness. Further, each cell has its own consciousness to a certain degree. We must remain aware of this cellular connection and the living nature of our universe.

11

Some Typical Problems and Treatments

A BULLET TO THE Heart. An eye doctor from Bavaria had constant stitches or sharp pains in the heart area. An EKG couldn't confirm the problem from a medical point of view, but the pain persisted. Gerhard performed an operation on the aura and removed a bullet he found in the heart. After the aura surgery, the pain disappeared.

Scars From an Aura Operation. A sixty-eight-year-old woman from Landshut had arthritis in both knees. After an aura operation, a scar was visible for two days. Since that time, there has been no more problem.

Arterial Implant. Because of a blocked artery, a woman from Regensburg planned to undergo a heart operation. An aura operation was carried out, where a piece of artery was implanted. That evening as she was preparing for bed, she noticed a fleck of blood on the inside of her bra at the exact spot of the operation. Since that time, she has had no more problems of that nature, and the planned operation never took place.

Disk Implant. Ian, age fifty-nine, from Aberfeldy, Scotland, had a problem with an intervertebral disk. The old disk was removed in the aura surgery, and a new one was transplanted. He was then able to bend over and touch the floor without pain. This was the first aura surgery and healing to be videotaped.

Drug Experimentation. A woman from Munich came to see Gerhard because of ongoing problems with her liver. Gerhard found an earthbound soul in the aura. At the same time, he could smell freshly cut wood and see an image of a tree that had been chopped down. From that experience, Gerhard felt that this earthbound soul had tried to experience an expansion of her consciousness with an extract from this tree trunk, resulting in an overdose and death. The poison worked on the liver and carried over to the woman in this life. She had extreme pain when pressure was put on the liver point. After freeing the earthbound soul, this point was free of pain.

Electrical Shock. A victim of execution by electric chair had many disturbances and sensitivity to her nervous system, with severe headaches and pain in the wrists and ankles. Gerhard treated this by removing the electrodes symbolically from the head, hands, and feet. He then released the bands around the chest, wrists, and ankles. After he finished, he advised the patient to drink a lot of water for the rest of her life because the inner organs had been burned. With this treatment, the problem was resolved for the lady, and she suffers much less.

Hangings and Garrotes. Many chronic problems in the neck and throat area were caused by executions of innocent people in previous lives. After aura surgery to remove ropes and garrotes, the pain disappears totally. At the same time, the backbone, neck, and collarbone area must be treated and returned to their proper positions.

Phantom Pain. A fifty-four-year-old man from Landshut had a leg amputated at the knee five years prior to his appointment with Gerhard. He suffered phantom pain in the missing leg. Gerhard found that the nerve ends were open in the aura. After an operation to splice the nerve ends, the gentleman has been pain free.

Venom. People who died of snakebite or spider bite in a past life frequently suffer problems of joint pain. The poison must be removed from the liver before the patient can recover. This means that the venom is present in the aura even though it cannot be detected in the physical body. This is not treatable with normal medical procedures since modern medicine cannot detect such a problem.

In general, he must remove the cause that remains in the aura (knife, bullet, poison) and suture any wounds in the aura before it is cleaned. Sometimes, he injects spiritual medicine, which flows into a hypodermic needle held in front of his forehead. When the proper dosage is injected, he can no longer feel any pressure in the needle. He uses a fresh needle for each injection. He has a large collection of knives, needles, thread, scissors, keys, and various other tools. It's always a bit stunning to see him operate, and even more exciting to see people's faces when they respond to the investigation, feel the effects of his unorthodox treatment, and finally experience the healing that takes place in their bodies.

Philosophy of Healing

Gerhard had learned to put his hands into the aura, he had felt the pain of his patients, and he has cured many of them and helped many more. He has given a great deal of thought to what is happening and is still trying to understand the nature of disease, injury, and healing.

Gerhard thinks if healing is possible, then it will take place. If a person is not helped by a healing, it could be that he is not the right healer for this person. It's a matter of empathy and resonance. The healer must resonate with the person who needs the healing. Sometimes, it could be that that the person needs another healing method. Astrology can be very important sometimes. A person can learn his potential and how it can be applied at that moment. When a person is tired or depressed and when Saturn is very close to his sun, then he knows that this is the reason and that it will end in a few months or half a year. This gives people hope because they know they can see an end and that the pain or depression won't last much longer. When you have the pain, you have the feeling that the pain will never end. If someone tells you it will be over, then it's easier to bear.

Illness and disease may occur for a number of reasons.

Accidental. It has been said that there's no such thing as an accident, but sometimes injuries or illness happen for no obvious reason. Due to carelessness or inattention, one can damage the physical body. Using the energy in the aura as a pattern, the body can heal itself in the same way that it was created. Children recover from their injuries quickly because their auras still remember how the physical body was created. As we mature in our bodies and lose touch with the source of healing, we forget how to heal ourselves. It takes us longer as we get older because we're not using the healing energy we're all born with.

Behavioral. Alcohol or drug abuse, smoking, and destructive or risky behavior (e.g., living with an abusive partner) may cause injury or illness. This can be healed, but the condition will return if the behavior is not altered. New patterns must be adopted.

Congenital. If someone is born with a disease or malformation, it can be said to be karmic. The entity has selected this condition for a life challenge or in order to help another entity meet a life challenge. This condition may also be present because the person has suffered a traumatic death and has reincarnated too quickly. This person may not respond permanently to a healing if the condition is necesssary for soul growth. However, a healing will take place if the healing itself is a part of the life plan! In other words, the person has to experience illness or disease before he can experience a healing.

An interesting thing about Gerhard is that he remains an involved and interested observer in the healings he conducts and never at any time feels that he is anything more than an instrument or a tool in this mysterious process. He doesn't claim to have any special powers or gifts other than being open to a power source that flows through his hands and body to the person in need of a healing. He believes that healing energy is channeled through his body, much like electricity from the outlet in the wall. He never considers himself the source of any healing energy. He feels he only has to remain "clean" in his own energy and thoughts, and that this healing power will continue to manifest through him. He's not a smoker, and while he is not a teetotaler, he never drinks alcohol if he will participate in a healing session the next day.

At an early stage in his healing career, he would pray for a healing to take place. He doesn't do that anymore. Now, before he begins to heal, he thanks God instead for the healing that has already taken place. He says, "When I give thanks for the healing, then I know that the healing has already taken place."

He always tells his clients that the expression of gratitude is more important than waiting for a healing to happen.

When he was a boy, he was very interested in religion, but he didn't understand about spirituality. His first contact with spirituality was when he met Tom Johanson, a famous healer from Great Britain. It was then that he had his first experience of feeling the energy in his hands and he could support the philosophy of Tom Johanson. It was then clear that one could have spiritual yearnings and express those outside of the influence of a particular organized religion.

When he started healing, he learned to hold his hands on the body and pray. He then learned to hold his hands in the aura. When he first came to Great Britain in 1989, a medium told him that the meeting with Tom Johanson had been a very important event because Tom had given him the key that he needed to unlock the doors of spiritual healing, and that was to be Gerhard's mission in life. If he used that key, then he would learn healing, but the method of healing he would eventually use would be very different than that used by Tom. Gerhard waited to see what that method might be.

It was seven years later when he met Stephen Turoff, a spiritual surgeon from Great Britain who performed surgery in the aura. It was at that point that Gerhard's healing methods changed, along with his thoughts about spiritualists and spiritualism. He discovered that it wasn't necessary to use his own energy to effect a healing. He feels that the spirit doctors are working behind him and through him, but he is not in a trance. He is fully conscious at all times. He can sometimes talk while he is healing and tells people what he finds or feels. Therefore, he is not like some other spiritual healers, who may have had psychic or spiritual experiences since childhood, where they saw and talked with spirits. This was not the case with Gerhard at all. He had no visions, mystical experiences, or dreams where he was told what his mission would be or shown anything in a paranormal sense. Furthermore, no one in his family, mother's side or father's side, ever did anything of this nature. His religious training and upbringing actually militated against him ever becoming a healer or medium or spiritualist.

It would be very helpful if a psychically gifted child could receive training in mediumship or clairvoyance while still in childhood. Gerhard feels that his healing powers were always present; they just needed his attention and desire in order to develop. We all have the possibility or potential for healing ourselves and others. It's possible for anyone to start learning to heal at any time if there is a sincere interest and dedication to this goal.

As for karmic things like nooses or bullets, which are often found in the aura, those are things which belong to a past life. It wasn't possible at the time of the injury for the person to understand or accept the events in that life. This lack of understanding or acceptance made it very difficult to absorb at the unconscious level. Memories were then stored in the person's energy field and carried with them to the next life.

It appears that emotions are the glue that make these karmic impressions or memories. There they remain, and they will not go away until a healing takes place, which involves understanding, forgiveness, and love. They will continue to work in the aura, and the person will continue to experience and repeat the negative patterns. If this experience and the emotional impact can be reenacted and understood on a conscious level as being true, then at this moment, a release of the memories can occur, resulting in a healing.

Frequently, people will react with great emotion to these revelations. Some people will learn, for example, that a chronic condition was caused by being hanged in a previous life. The natural reaction is, "Who did that to me—why did that happen?" They may ask for details. These people are very much into playing the part of victim, repeating over and over, "Why?"

A typical example is an American woman who was very upset to learn that some of her physical problems in this life had been caused by a hanging. She demanded to know if it was her present-day sister who had done the deed! She even sent a letter to Gerhard later, requesting more details of this long-ago crime and her sister's involvement. She couldn't profit from the healing because of her continued suspicion and lack of forgiveness and love. She could not lose her need to blame others!

Gerhard must then explain that it isn't important to know the personalities involved or the reason for that death, only to extend love and forgiveness to the persons who committed the act, to yourself for whatever role you played in bringing that action to you, and to God for allowing it to happen. The first step in healing is acknowledgment and acceptance of the condition. Sometimes, people have to be reminded that they may have played the roles of master and of servant or slave. If you can imagine being a slave in a previous life, then you must also imagine the position of owning slaves and having the responsibility, and karmic burden, of being a master over another's fate.

The aura is like a shell around the body, and all of these karmic experiences have an impact on the aura. Gerhard describes the aura as covered with dirt and damage, similar to an automobile that is involved in an accident. The damage from the collision won't be seen clearly until the automobile has been washed and inspected. It's possible then to see the color and make of the car. Only then can an assessment be made of the necessary repairs. In the same vein, if you have a car and you know that a part is corroded or dirty, you have to clean it up before you can fully check the function of that part.

It's the same thing with the aura. You have to take away the karmic soil in the aura, and then it will be possible to see and feel the present condition of the body more clearly. Before a physical healing can take place, the karmic residue has to be removed. Gerhard regards an aura healing as similar to washing the car. After the karmic dirt has been removed, he can begin to work on healing any present life conditons.

Dr. Brian Weiss is a well-known author and psychother-apist, and in his book, *Messages from the Masters*, he says:

> When we remove the outer layers of dirt and debris, the negative thoughts and emotions, when we clean and polish away the outer overlay, then we can once again discern the true diamonds we really are. We are immortal and divine souls on our way home. We have always been diamonds underneath.

He was referring to the emotions and attitudes people hold that are negative and hurtful. Those same words can be applied to the aura cleansing and repairs that Gerhard believes are necessary for physical well-being.

Temporary Healings and Permanent Healings

One puzzling aspect of working with healers is trying to determine why some people receive a full and complete healing with lasting effects and others are only healed tem-porarily with symptoms returning wholly or in part at a later date. One wonders if the healing was only a tem-porary hypnotic effect. It's altogether too easy to say that the patient really didn't want a healing or couldn't accept a healing at that time. Gerhard believes that the etheric body may have many layers of emotion and injuries that are being carried and expressed in the physical. It would be akin to peeling an onion. If you attack only one layer at a time, it could take quite some time to remove all the layers of pain and suffering.

I used to have some problem with my heart. Some-times, it would seem irregular, jumping around with tight-ness in my chest. I never had the symptoms of a full heart attack, but the wild heartbeat would frighten me. These attacks were irregular but happened about twice a year. I consulted a heart specialist once many years ago in El Paso, and he diagnosed a mitral valve prolapse, but no treatment was ever given, and it only happened occasionally. Many years later, in Arizona, my family physician diagnosed what he called a heart murmur and asked that I have my heart checked with a specialist in Tucson. I called the heart specialist and made an appointment. Before the appointment, however, I experienced a wild irregular heartbeat one evening. I was in bed at the time and got frightened, especially as I thought about the upcoming appointment. My entire chest was hurting, and my husband was concerned enough to consider calling for an ambulance.

I asked him to call Gerhard instead.

Even though it was the middle of the night in Arizona, I knew that Gerhard would be working in his office in Germany. Franz telephoned him, and Gerhard promised to send his spirit physicians to me immediately. It wasn't immediate enough for me ... they seemed to arrive about fifteen minutes later. I felt them enter the room. There seemed to be two or three energies in attendance, one standing by my shoulder, at least one standing at the foot of the bed, and perhaps a third energy in between. They set to work right away, and I could feel what seemed to be fingers in the middle of my chest, moving something about. About ten minutes later, I felt an instant relaxation in my chest. The heartbeat was again regular, and I was relaxed. The tightness in my chest disappeared. It seemed as if something inside my chest just released.

My stress test with the heart specialist failed to produce a single symptom of heart problems, and my family physician has not detected the murmur since. I don't know if it's been repaired, but I haven't had one instance of an irregular heartbeat since that night five years ago. Even though I don't have any documentation about this condition, whatever it was, the symptoms have never resurfaced. This was a healing for me.

An illness or symptom creates a pattern. It is not dissimilar to learning to play a musical instrument. In order to play, it's necessary to practice, practice, practice. The rhythms or patterns must be repeated until they can be performed automatically, without thought or attention from the player. It's similar to driving a car. When you are learning to drive, you have to think about the brake pedal and the accelerator and the turn signal. After driving a few years, everything is automatic. The hands and feet know what to do! You only have to think about where you should turn and when you should change lanes. You make the decision, and the hands and feet react and carry out the decision. A professional or skilled musician only must think about the music he wants to play, and the hands will play those patterns. Once learned, those skills remain on the hard drive, so to speak. The only sticking point here is that if one has developed bad driving habits or bad playing habits, they also become permanent! They're permanently inscribed on our behavior patterns, and changing those patterns is very difficult.

An alcoholic who wants to break his drinking habit must also break other habits and learn new ones. Sometimes, this is a difficult process, but it's not impossible. Old friendships and associations must be dropped and new ones made. It's a fact that sometimes a recovering alcoholic who has successfully dropped his drinking habits or abusive behavior will end up in divorce court! The long-suffering spouse who has been the victim of mental and physical abuse may not be able to relate successfully to the new person with a different character. The new behavior patterns may create an environment where the former alcoholic may not be able to fulfill the needs of a spouse who is accustomed to and relatively comfortable with one kind of action and reaction.

First, we have to acknowledge that every living person has an aura, an energy field which is vibrating around him. This energy field will disappear from the human form upon death. This energy field is shaped roughly like the human form, and the inner organs are mirrored in this energy field. Eastern religious thought holds that this energetic body has many layers which can be labeled:

1. etheric, which shows the physical condition and health of the physical body;

2. emotional, which shows the feelings of the person;

3. mental, which shows thoughts and mental processes;

4. astral, which shows the bridge between the physical world and the spiritual world;

5. etheric template, which is supposed to hold the etheric aura in place and holds the pattern for the etheric aura;

6. celestial, which connects to the world of the spirit; and

7. ketheric template, which is the golden eggshell that surrounds and protects the individual and the six layers of the aura.

The energy field, or perhaps only the etheric template, has actually been responsible for creation and formation of the physical body, although conventional scientific thought might postulate that the chemical and electrical components of the physical body have created this magnetic field, and not the reverse!

When Gerhard is manipulating the energy in the aura or is injecting spiritual medicine, people report that they are able to feel these motions or the prick of a needle, even when they can't observe what he is doing. These are the same feelings and sensations that might be experienced in an actual operation. This means that the aura has a connection to the nervous system of the body and also to the consciousness.

There is a way to subjectively prove that information is actually stored in the aura. Past life patterns and memories can be uncovered even when people are storing the information of the execution or traumatic death in their auras, and reacting to it, hundreds of years later.

That means that when Gerhard draws his finger across the throat area, the person may feel pain or a pulling sensation. This is the indication that the information of the knife or executioner's blade is still stored in that person's aura. Another person would have no reaction whatsoever to the finger being drawn across the throat area.

For example, Gerhard may detect a blockage in the aura surrounding a person's shoulder. He may pinch his fingers together and pull in the area where he feels the blockage. When that motion is detected or felt by the subject, then Gerhard has an idea of the size or texture of the object. He might then take his tweezers or a larger instrument, or even use both hands, and pull the object out of the aura. The proof is in the reaction. He is then able to test if the object is gone by repeating the earlier motions. If nothing is felt, then there is no negative memory pattern remaining in the aura. It can be said the the operation is complete. In this way, Gerhard has removed bullets, arrows, spears, and other projectiles from the aura's energy field. The result is almost always pain relief and improved mobility.

Any pain or damage to the physical body in an earlier life can be stored in the aura. It appears that the most damage occurs when the injury or trauma has an emotional impact. That's the reason that forgiveness of the "crime" or injustice in the earlier life is so important. If the emotional connection can't be broken, then the physical symptoms may remain or return.

The point is that if information is indeed stored in the aura, then it's possible to remove or alter (reprogram) it. We can say that the aura is like the hard drive on a computer. It's only a matter of being able to read the information stored there. It is a novel idea that the information can be recalled and then treated, like removing a virus from your software.

If you have a flash drive or CD on which music or information is stored, the CD or drive alone will not be useful. The information is available but cannot be accessed. It will, in fact, be meaningless to one who doesn't know its potential. In addition, you must have a CD player or a computer or some other medium to release or recall the information or music which is recorded there. (The operating word here is *medium*.) Give a brand-new CD to a native in a remote jungle, and it doesn't matter what fine symphonic music by the world's greatest artists may be stored on that shiny little disc. He might only be able to hang it on a rawhide thong around his neck and think it a fine ornament.

The important difference, of course, is that the CD alone can do no harm or have no effect, no matter what information is stored on it. Without the means to release the information and some understanding of how it was stored, it will be forever locked up. A CD by itself can even be useful as a toy, tool, garden decoration, coaster, and so on. The information stored in our auras, however, is active! That hard drive in our aura is being activated all day and every day. It never sleeps. That information, positive and negative, has a daily and regular effect on our bodies and minds! We must listen to the music from our past lives, unharmonious as it may be. Most of us aren't even aware that the music is playing. This information stored in our auras is powerfully charged with emotion. We can even say that emotions write the programs for us. The only way we have at the present time to reach this stored material is through extrasensory methods. Psychic readings, tarot cards, astrology, mediumship, and dreams are some of the ways we can try to reach this material, which we believe to be stored in the subconscious.

It makes one wonder if there might be a reader someday that reads that information and plays it back on command. You will then have your soul's history to read like a book. Does this sound like another Eastern idea—the Akashic Records?

The concepts that the aura exists, that information is stored in the aura, and that a gifted psychic might be able to recover that information and change it leads to the conclusion that life never ends, that life is energy, that information is energy, and that energy is never lost or forgotten. We're adding to this information every day of our lives, even while we're sleeping and dreaming! We are running our programs all the time.

The base teachings of most religions are that they were founded and created directly by God and handed down somehow to mankind. Some of these teachings may not be valid or useful at this stage of development. The responsibility of religion is to find a way to bring truth to the people.

Gerhard believes that the two greatest errors in our relationship to God are that God has forsaken us, or that he wants to punish us for not giving him what he needs.

The truth is that life does not end with what we call death. Life can no longer be viewed as a random and unique occurrence, with the circumstances and conditions of our birth being blind fortune (or misfortune). Events aren't random, either, but can be seen as a natural result of our thoughts and decisions over many lives.

In the same way, we cannot limit our responsibility and blame our condition on someone else's negative energies, on our parents, on our race or color, on evil spirits, or on the devil! We are placed in our current condition by our actions and choices today and in past incarnations. It is our responsibility to make the best of it, overcome it, and help others along the way.

Why Healing Takes Place and Why It Doesn't

It would be the greatest folly if we believed that every person and every problem could be healed with simple aura surgery.

Every illness has its own reason. This applies to traditional medicine also; it's a fact that each person reacts differently to a treatment or medication. One medication could be a miracle treatment for one person and have absolutely no effect on another. It might even be dangerous for a third person because every human being is not constructed the same way. The problem is not with the medication. The law of resonance is in play here. Only the medication that resonates with the individual's biological, mental, and emotional composition will be effective. To put it simply, body, mind, and soul must be in agreement, and the treatment or medication must resonate with the person.

For this reason, we need many medications and many different healing methods in order to effectively treat the variety of individuals who need attention. No one has invented a "magic bullet" yet that works for everyone. Many musicians with a variety of instruments are required for the symphony orchestra to blend the differing sounds to create the full harmony and beauty when they all come together.

So it is the art of healing to discover which therapy will perfectly resonate with the one in need of help.

Healing cannot be forced. It must be offered and accepted. Healing begins not with the healer, but with the one who seeks the healing. The doctor or healer can only support or guide the self-healing process. In order for this to really happen, old blocks at the emotional level must often be cleared.

In principle, our bodies cannot be ill. Each cell wants to function at an optimal level, and each cell carries within itself its own design and intelligence for a self-healing program. It is very similar to a computer in that the best hardware and most expensive computer will not function at all unless the software is correctly programmed and a virus or worm has not invaded the process! Is it a problem of civilization that the perfectly programmed cells have received new programming and information radically different from our original design?

In my experience, these programs are located in the hypothalamus, in the limbic system, between the right and left sides of the brain. Because life has neither a beginning nor an ending, old memory patterns from past lives or blockages can have an impact on the program in the morphogenetic field. Rupert Sheldrake was one of the first scientists who could prove that human beings and animals are all linked in a morphogenetic field. An individual may desire a healing very much, but the illness cannot be healed for some unknown reason. That reason might be an emotional program that prevents a healing from taking place. It could be that the person himself is unable to release or let go of the disease.

A little joke might provide an example of what is meant here. Jesus Christ visited a hospital and found three men sitting on a couch in the waiting room.

Jesus asked the first man, "My son, what is wrong with you?"

The man responded that his arm was broken and he was suffering. Jesus then blessed the arm, and he was healed. The man felt his arm was whole again, and he left the hospital thanking the Lord for the healing.

Jesus then came to the second man and asked him the same question.

"I've broken my leg, and I can't walk," said the man.

Jesus then blessed the leg, and he was instantly healed.

"I can walk again!" said the man. "Thank you, Jesus!" The man sprang to his feet and ran out of the hospital.

Jesus then came to the last man on the sofa and asked him the same question. "My son, what is wrong with you?"

The man responded, "I have a most horrible pain in my back, but please don't heal me now, because I'm on paid sick leave for six weeks!"

When an illness or disease serves a purpose for someone, it is very difficult to heal them, regardless of which healing method is brought to the problem. The healing will not be successful. It is not always necessary that the patient believe in the healer's methods, but it is absolutely essential that he trust the therapist.

Very often during or after a healing, people feel no change at all, especially the first day, the first week, or even some months later. The time must be ripe for the healing to be effective. Often, there must be an emotional shift before the healing fully manifests. No one can accurately predict when and how this will occur. How often does it happen that people with incurable illnesses receive spontaneous healing with the power of prayer alone? There are innumerable cases, and they are called miracles. Others may pray night and day and receive no healing at all. Does it depend on a god who decides whether we are healthy or not? I don't believe so. If God is love, then it is an unconditional love. It is a love that we cannot define or explain, and it is for everyone, without exception—a love that we cannot explain with words.

But we can feel this love when the brain turns off and our consciousness becomes quiet. Then, the heart can open, and we might hear what our body is saying to us.

Our bodies speak to us with pictures and emotions, not words. If we are able to hear what our bodies are saying, we might understand what we need to do in order to be healthy again. Illness is often an escape from the everyday world of family, business, labor, and obligations. Illness is an opportunity to be silent and listen to your body.

12

Oaths and Vows

Much learning does not teach understanding.
—Heraclitus

BE CAREFUL OF AN oath or vow that will bind you for all
eternity. Do not take it lightly, for our souls know and
accept that eternity is eternal. Every cell in our body knows
this and accepts it also.

A vow or oath taken in a previous lifetime may have
impressed a duty upon our souls that is still taken very
seriously at the highest level. It does not matter at all if
the oath is not consciously recalled. Every cell in the body
recalls the oath, and it's imprinted on the energy field. The
words "I swear" will impress a pattern on the thyroid gland
because they are spoken aloud. The thyroid gland is linked
to the adrenal gland; therefore, the pattern may manifest in
the adrenal gland as well. Gerhard will typically detect this
blockage at the throat, and he will ask mental test questions. A mental question might be, "Are there any oaths
or vows involved?" This memory pattern could manifest

as a thyroid imbalance, blood pressure problems, or heart rhythm irregularities.

What are eternal vows? Traditional marriage vows spoken in the church before a religious authority, the family, friends, and community did not require an eternal vow. One vows only to be faithfully married—"til death do us part." This is a reasonable vow in light of our limited life span on earth. Of course, these vows are spoken more casually now than in the past, but they are still only for a lifetime. This is not an eternal vow. A mere promise of eternal love in the midst of a warm embrace will surely not cause trouble in future lives, but a formal vow or solemn oath made under serious circumstances will be impressed upon the energy field and remain until it is appropriately released or fulfilled.

In particular, eternal vows taken in formal ceremonies or rituals are the dangerous ones. These are the vows and oaths that are imprinted with religious or fraternal over-tones and reinforced with deep emotion and commitment. Dire consequences will result if they are broken.

Mostly, the vows or oaths taken in prior lifetimes will manifest as irrational fears regarding money or love rela-tionships. It will also create a feeling of not being worthy of success or love if one has taken a vow of self-sacrifice in the past. Of all the vows and oaths, the five most powerful ones are 1. chastity, 2. poverty, 3. servitude, 4. eternal love, and 5. ceremonial.

Vow of Chastity. Nuns and priests routinely take vows of chastity and forswear any sexual conduct whatsoever, including self-pleasure. For all eternity! A nun cannot visu-alize a sexual relationship or bringing a child into the world because either act would violate the vow of chastity.

Vow of Poverty. An example of an eternal vow is the vow of poverty required by a religion to enter an order.

Priests and nuns take such vows and order their lives around non-materialism and self-sacrifice. Accumulation of wealth would be an abomination to a person who has taken such a vow. This would certainly keep material wealth away from the door! The individual may have a conscious desire for money and strive night and day, but the goal will elude him because he is truly unable to visualize being rich and will never be able to attain a goal that cannot be visualized.

Vow of Servitude. Many people in ancient times had to take a vow of servitude to a master or ruler. Charlemagne required that members of his court take a vow of service for all eternity. An individual who has taken this vow may be unable to spend money or time on himself and may appear to be an unselfish and caring person to his friends and family. The problem with the vow to serve Charlemagne is that in order to serve him faithfully, he must be incarnated at the same time and place. The vow to serve others must be fulfilled, and Charlemagne might not be incarnated at the same time.

Vow of Eternal Love. This sounds great in romance novels but will not work out over many lifetimes. If you're waiting for that one you promised to love forever in the seventeenth century, you might be very lonely in this one! You might find new relationships, but the inability to make a commitment to someone new will place too much of an emotional handicap on the relationship, which will always be unsatisfactory.

Ceremonial Vows and Oaths. These are important because they were undertaken with a great deal of ritual and symbolism, which will leave a deep imprint on the consciousness.

Other oaths and vows might include those of silence, loyalty, revenge, damnation, self-castigation, revenge, or blood bonds. They may or may not be issues in this lifetime, but it would depend on the circumstances and seriousness of the oaths when they were taken.

Eternal self-damnation and self-castigation are similar, being practiced by some religious devotees who use whips, chains, thorns, and so on, in order to punish themselves.

Blood bonds. Although this does not come up very often, it may also create physical or emotional problems for some people. Participation in a ceremony requiring an oath and exchange of blood is especially serious because it involves cooperation and commitment at several levels. It may start with a ceremony involving secret meetings, candles and music, presence of others, spoken vows, and reinforcement with an exchange of vital fluids, especially blood. This evokes images of black magic. Not quite so sinister but just as powerful are the blood brother rituals undertaken by North American Indians. This is an important commitment to another individual that might not be possible to maintain in a new lifetime where the brother is not present.

Some Examples of Eternal Oaths Still in Effect

Gerhard tells a story of a businessman he met in Europe. He was the managing director of a large underwriting firm that specializes in what we know in America as initial public offerings (IPOs). These are usually undertaken when a small private company wants to sell stock and become a publicly traded firm and needs an influx of new capital for expansion purposes. This gentleman was extremely successful in helping small companies make this step toward becoming larger and more profitable. However, he noted that when his firm tried to help an already large and successful firm grow even larger and more successful, the firm met with disappointment and failure and lost money in the process. The failures resulted for many different reasons, so it was impossible to pinpoint any mistake or failure at the underwriting level. The company which had hired his servcies would unexpectedly fall into bankruptcy, the owner would die, or the market would change, all of which could not be foreseen at the time of the IPO.

The businessman had consulted Gerhard for a thyroid problem, and Gerhard believed that he had undertaken a voluntary vow of poverty in a past life. That vow now restricted him professionally and created a block to any success this man might enjoy in any occupation. An unfulfilled oath from a prior lifetime typically manifests as a thyroid insufficiency or illness caused by thyroid failure. The information of that vow was stored in the thyroid gland because it was a spoken vow. That vow of poverty would allow him to earn his livelihood but would not permit him to prosper and become wealthy. He would always be stymied by his vow of poverty.

After Gerhard completed his treatment, the businessman was able to let go of the vow of poverty and move on to great success with larger firms and major corporations. Today, he thanks Gerhard for the prosperity and wealth he is now enjoying. He is truly reaping the financial benefits he'd earned with his hard work.

In a second case, a thirty-three-year-old woman consulted Gerhard for her infertility. She and her husband had been married for ten years and were unable to produce the family they both desired. The doctors had found no reason for the failure to conceive, and the couple were otherwise healthy individuals, but no baby was forthcoming.

In consulting with the woman, Gerhard asked her to imagine that she was walking down the street and saw a pregnant woman approaching. What would she do? How would she feel? She replied immediately that she would feel horror to see the pregnant woman on the street and would cross to the other side to avoid her. She was not comfortable with this question at all. When she was a young girl, she said she was repulsed by pregnancy and could not be around a pregnant female at all. Gerhard knew that she had probably been a nun in at least one lifetime and taken a vow of chastity. That vow was still stored in the memory pattern and was still active and in full force and effect. Her conscious desire for a family could not be realized because of the prior oath of chastity. (Visualize a pregnant nun, and you'll understand her horror.) Even though the physical body was able to become pregnant and produce a child, the subconscious self was repeating the mantra, "No, I'm a nun!" This vow could not be violated.

Gerhard has developed a technique wherein the soul is allowed to release itself from voluntary vows taken in a past life that have become undesirable or troublesome in this lifetime. It's a complicated process but not impossible. If the person is ready to change his life, it can be accomplished. Gerhard would like to train more therapists in this multiphase process, which involves several levels of therapy.

13

Earthbound Souls

GERHARD OFTEN FINDS EARTHBOUND souls while he is feeling auras. They can affect our health and mental well-being in negative ways. Gerhard refers to the film *Ghost* as being a good film example of an earthbound entity. The ghost in the film was concerned about some unfinished business before he could move into the light.

Earthbound souls are very easy to locate in a person's aura and usually not too difficult to remove. The entity may only be confused and remain as a refugee with the unsuspecting host. It may not even cause much trouble for the host. However, more frequently, the entity is frightened, is unaware that he has passed, or has an urgent reason to remain on the earth plane. Very sensitive or psychic individuals may be more likely to be victimized by an earthbound, but this isn't always the case. Hospitals, battleground sites, and disaster scenes hold very strong psychic imprints and may also harbor some lost souls.

There are many reasons why a soul may become trapped in our world instead of moving on to the next plane of existence.

When a person dies unexpectedly or as a result of some great injustice, the shock and emotion of the passing may cause the entity to become earthbound. A suicide or murder victim is very likely to become earthbound because of the violence of the passing. Gerhard believes that a criminal who was guilty and punished by execution would probably not become earthbound because there was a karmic balance in the crime and the punishment. The soul accepts his punishment and understands the reason for his death.

However, it could be that an earthbound spirit might remain on this plane as a result of being executed for a crime he didn't commit. The entity might feel pain, anger, sadness, outrage, or any number of emotions that keep it connected to the material world.

An entity may have died violently or unexpectedly and may have been totally unprepared for that experience. The entity might not be able to make a connection spiritually with the helpers from the other side or to see the help or light that's being sent to him. He is like a horse with blinders that can only have a limited view. Imagine an old phonograph record with a break in the groove that repeats a word or phrase over and over until the needle is moved. For the reader who doesn't remember phonograph records, it's like a computer program that isn't responding even though the program is running on the desktop.

A person who is unable to control his passion for drugs, alcohol, sex, gambling, or some other pursuit he enjoyed on this plane might not want to leave, preferring to stay here and seek those experiences to which he was addicted in life.

We wonder if some people are too frightened to move into the next plane, particularly if they aren't spiritually prepared or feel that they have committed too many sins or made too many mistakes to go to heaven, preferring to stay here rather than go home and face the music of what they perceive as Judgment Day.

How do they come in?

An earthbound can only come in if the aura is open. The aura can be opened in a number of ways.

Hospitalization. Hospitalization after major surgery is one way for the aura to be vulnerable to possession by an earthbound. A patient whose consciousness is suppressed or depressed by medication, anesthesia, or low energy levels may be a prime target for an earthbound. The body (with its energy field) has been laid open on an operating room table with no spiritual or psychic protection. Since the hospital is also the location for trauma cases and deathbed crises, there are plenty of earthbound souls roaming about. Surgery creates an opportunity for an earthbound to share a physical body with another being. In other words, nobody's watching the store!

Alcohol and/or Drugs. Another way is when the living person is in a drugged or drunken state by choice. Someone who is addicted to alcohol, tobacco, drugs, or even sex is not in control of his body or soul and is open to outside influences. He is also reinforcing his own negative karmic patterns.

Occult Practices. Some people definitely open themselves up to an earthbound entity when they experiment with Ouija boards, tarot cards, crystal balls, and séances without proper education and development. The first step in psychic development is psychic protection. In their eagerness to develop psychic gifts, obtain nirvana, or be one with the universe—or even just to get some laughs—they may be opening their energy fields up to a very undesirable experience.

Negative Emotions. Anger, revenge, hatred, or despair may lead to an emotional state where the aura is open and unprotected.

Undeveloped and Unrecognized Mediumship. I've never read any estimates as to what percentage of the population may have unrecognized mediumship abilities, but it may be higher than we think. This is an entirely human and normal ability and many people may have more mediumship ability than they know. Our culture is not generally open to expressions of mediumship in our everyday life, in spite of the popularity of mediumship in movies and television programming, i.e. *The Ghost Whisperer, Medium, Crossing Over.* Just as some people have better singing voices than others, some people may be more plugged in to the universe and possess ESP and mediumship than is generally thought. Most people admit to strange experiences from time to time, and most people believe in these things in spite of the negative press, hostility from organized religion, and denials to the contrary. If a person is sensitive or possesses mediumistic powers, the aura may be brighter and more attractive to an entity seeking expression. They are drawn to one who has the ability to sense their presence. If one has these abilities and doesn't recognize them or acknowledge them, then there is no preparation or understanding of what could occur. If a person possesses these abilities, it would be better to acknowledge them and train the psyche to receive and understand the messages. If not, the resulting experiences could only be frightening and threatening.

Earthbound at the Pearl Harbor Memorial

During a demonstration healing in Tucson, Arizona, Gerhard found an earthbound entity in the aura of a young man who was a student at the University of Arizona. The entity didn't respond to Gerhard's initial efforts to remove it and remained stubborn through several efforts.

Finally, Gerhard attempted to psychically contact the

earthbound and received an impression of the Pearl Harbor Memorial in Hawaii. He asked the young man, "Have you recently visited the Pearl Harbor Memorial?"

"No," he responded, "not recently. My family took me there when I was eight years old."

Gerhard returned to the entity and got an impression that he desired some kind of recognition or validation. Gerhard got the impression of the entity's name, which he then told to the group. The entity apparently didn't understand that he had passed over. Gerhard received the impression that the entity had remained at Pearl Harbor after the attack until he found the open energy of the visiting boy. He had simply been a hitchhiker since then. Gerhard didn't feel that this entity had actually harmed the young man but may have drained his energy at times. This was confirmed by the subject, who said that he frequently felt low energy and tired for no reason.

The group helped Gerhard in sending love to the earthbound entity along with a group blessing. We directed him to "look for the light" and join his friends and loved ones that had waited for him so long. This kind of experience is always quite moving, as other members of the group often report feeling this great love and homecoming joy in the room.

A Toast to Napoleon

Gerhard has a very close connection with Hermann, and they have had many interesting experiences together. One of the more bizarre experiences occurred during one of Gerhard's workshops in Lubeck. Hermann complained that something was wrong with his right arm and that he had a most unusual feeling there. Gerhard felt in the aura of the arm and sensed that his right arm was indeed damaged. Hermann said that two weeks prior to doing this workshop, he had experienced pain and numbness in this arm. Gerhard felt the aura had the impression that the arm was like the arm of a soldier, but it was very badly damaged, almost destroyed.

A picture of a French soldier emerged, one who had died in the northern part of Germany during Napoleon's return after he lost the battle in Russia in 1812. On that dreadful return trip with his army, many soldiers died because it was winter and they had nothing to eat. It was icy cold, and the soldier was lying on the ground, dying. Just before he closed his eyes for the last time, he saw the great Napoleon approaching on his horse-drawn sled. Napoleon rode swiftly by his fallen soldiers, glancing neither to the left nor to the right. He never let his gaze fall to the wounded and dying scattered in the ice and snow around him. In his eyes, they were all losers and failures, beneath his attention or pity.

The dying soldier was so traumatized and suffered such emotional hurt by this cold treatment that he couldn't find release after death. He became an earthbound spirit. This was the person that Gerhard now felt in Hermann's aura. He was earthbound and still disturbed after more than 180 years! Gerhard wanted to release this poor spirit immediately, but he had the feeling that he didn't want to do it in the workshop in front of the others; he wanted to do it later in Hermann's library.

After the workshop, they went into the library, and Gerhard removed his eyeglasses and shoes, as is his custom during a healing. He felt Hermann's aura again and readily found the soldier. He was released from Hermann's aura very, very easily. He had been truly ready to go. But his energy remained in the room with them.

Gerhard could hear his voice speaking to him. "Now, before I go home, we have to make a toast."

Gerhard told Hermann, "Please take that bottle there," and pointed at a bottle over on a table.

Without his glasses, Gerhard couldn't see which bottle he pointed to. Hermann picked up the bottle and brought it to Gerhard. It was a bottle of Napoleon brandy!

They made three toasts. One was for Hermann because he had hosted this soldier in his aura, one was for the healer, and one was for Napoleon! The soldier had finally forgiven Napoleon. The forgiveness made it possible for him to be released.

Because of this experience, Gerhard could readily understand why an entity passing under such difficult circumstances would store this information in his consciousness. It is abundantly clear that negative emotions will bind us to this world more than anything else.

Kristina Hears Voices

It happened in a workship in Lubeck A woman inquired if Gerhard could help her daughter, Kristina, who was hearing voices. The voices had encouraged her to rip a page out of a book at school. She tried to ignore the voices, but it wasn't possible. They didn't stop until she finally ripped out the page. Then, things were quiet, and the voices disappeared for several weeks. The voices had now returned, and she was constantly hearing them. She couldn't rest for the voices telling her what to do. Her family and teachers were very distraught and didn't know what to do.

At that time, Gerhard was staying with his friend Hermann. Kristina was brought to the house. Gerhard felt her aura and discovered what felt like an enormous, heavy bag on her back. He received the impression that there were three different entities, and she confirmed that she heard three different voices. He asked her to sit down, and he played a tape of Bach organ music at a very loud volume. He selected Toccata and Fugue in D Minor because the power of this music is like an electroshock for the aura and gives it an extremely strong vibration.

After the music ended, the entities were easily released, one at a time. When the last one was released, Kristina leaped out of her chair with excitement. Gerhard suggested that she go into the bathroom at once and take a shower. He felt it was necessary that she clean her entire body to match her clean aura, which was now free of entities for the first time in six months! She happily complied while Gerhard, her mother, and the other family members conversed in the living room. They could all hear her singing happily in the shower. This was very satisfying for Gerhard.

An Earthbound Voyeur at the Amusement Park

A very interesting case of a voyeuristic earthbound occurred in Europe. A woman had an appointment with Gerhard. In the scope of his examination, he found an earthbound in the aura.

He asked, "Do you sometimes have the feeling of being watched?"

"Yes," she replied, "especially when I'm showering or in the bathroom."

Gerhard then received a vivid image of a famous amusement park near Paris.

"Have you been on holiday in France?" he inquired.

"Yes," she replied. She paused and then exclaimed, "As a matter of fact, I remember that was the first time that I had the feeling that I was being watched. I was in the restroom at the park, and I got very uncomfortable with the feeling that I was being observed."

Gerhard then saw in the aura that a voyeur had suffered a heart attack in the ladies' restroom in the midst of his favorite pastime. His soul had then found an opportunity to attach itself to her and remained with her when she returned to Germany from her vacation. Gerhard was able to release the entity, who left quite easily after he was acknowledged.

A Voyeur in the Bedroom

About 2004, a woman who lived near Landshut asked Gerhard to perform a dowsing in her bedroom because she had recently felt that someone was watching her. In addition, her little dog wouldn't enter the bedroom even though his bed was located there. He had always slept in her room, and now he refused to enter.

When he came into the bedroom, Gerhard noticed a rattan chair and felt an energy there. He felt that someone was sitting in the chair—a man, leaning back in the chair with his legs crossed and his arms folded across his chest, very comfortable indeed.

Gerhard asked him, "What are you doing here?"

"I like to watch her undressing," the man responded.

Gerhard told him, "You are no longer in a material body; you are in a spirit form now."

"No, I am here, and I like it here."

Since he showed no willingness to move along, Gerhard decided to play some music on the stereo. He selected Toccata and Fugue in D Minor and began to play it. The music seemed to make the entity nervous, so Gerhard told him that he planned to turn up the volume. When he did just that, the entity became more agitated, so Gerhard turned it up again!

Gerhard then felt that the entity was ready to listen to him. He advised him to look up and around to see if there was another being in the area.

Gerhard quietly said, "They are waiting for you on the other side. You just have to release yourself to go with them." At that same moment, Gerhard felt the entity was gone.

The little dog immediately charged into the room with his tail wagging. He ran excitedly around the room and then bounded to his dog bed and snuggled down.

Gerhard's client excitedly asked him if she could call her friend and tell her what had happened.

She explained that her friend had recently made a short trip and had taken her dog with her. When she went back to the car to return home, the dog snarled and seemed reluctant to get in. The dog normally sat in the rear passenger seat behind the driver. This time, he was very anxious about getting into the car. The lady finally lifted him and pushed him into his usual place, but he scrambled over to a spot behind the passenger seat.

She started the motor, and at the same moment, her right foot seemed to be pushed down on the gas pedal, right to the floorboard. In spite of this, she could only pull forward very slowly and was afraid to shift to second. She drove home in first gear and was thankful that it was a short drive. She parked the car and was afraid to get in again. There was no obvious problem with the gas pedal or brake; the problem seemed to be the heavy pressure on her foot.

Gerhard agreed to give a consultation to the friend, and one hour later found himself sitting in the front passenger seat of the automobile. He had a feeling that someone was sitting behind the driver's seat. In his mind's eye, he saw a tall, slender man. When Gerhard asked him what he was doing there, he responded excitedly, "I'm a race car driver!"

Gerhard told him, "This is not a race car, and you are no longer in a material body. You don't need a race car." Again, he found it necessary to argue with the entity, who insisted that he was a race car driver.

Back to the Bach! (Pardon the pun.) As it turns out, Bach is very good for removing unwanted spirits. It seems to annoy and agitate them. Gerhard placed a CD in the car stereo and played a Bach composition at a very loud volume. After a few moments, he turned the volume down and tried again to communicate with the entity.

After a short time, Gerhard felt that the entity was ready to travel on to the spiritual world and helped effect the release. When Gerhard opened the door to leave, the dog jumped into the car and ran to his customary seat behind the driver, anxious to make a road trip again. All was well again.

Animals will sense the presence of an earthbound entity more readily than human beings. They are also sensitive to the emotions of the entity and will respond accordingly. The presence of a loving entity will affect the animal in a positive manner, with tail wagging and happy movements. A disruptive entity will affect the animal in an aggressive or fearful manner, depending on the disposition of the animal.

Invitation to an Earthbound Soul

At private demonstrations and at workshops, Gerhard often speaks to groups about earthbound entities. He tries to dispel popular notions of ghosts and demons and presents earthbound entities in a less negative way. People are surprised and sometimes frightened when he speaks of earthbound entities or discovers them in their auras. He teaches people how very easy it is to remove an earthbound from the auras of living persons affected by them. He again refers to the film *Ghost* as a good example.

Gerhard explains how earthbound spirits are able to interact with living persons and how they are able to influence our lives and activities.

Release of Earthbound Entities

Gerhard's technique to release earthbound entities involves sending unconditional love and forgiveness to the entity, asking for forgiveness from the entity for its removal from the aura or energy field of the unknowing host, and explaining to the entity that it must move on. The entity is asked to look around and up for the light and for friends or loved ones who wait to assist it. The waiting helpers have usually been waiting a long time to offer this help.

14

Slavery, Torture, Murders, Suicides, and Executions

Healing Past Life Injuries and Psychic Insults to the Aura

DURING PUBLIC DEMONSTRATIONS OF aura healing, Gerhard will focus on the head, neck, and chest areas. The reason for this is that it is usually less personal and almost everyone will benefit from a healing in this area. The result is that he will find a lot of victims of hangings and garrottes. If a pattern is found wherein the subject responds to movements in his aura, Gerhard will sometimes ask the question, "Could it be that you don't like Spanish culture?"

Nowadays, no one likes to admit to prejudice, so there's always a bit of hesitation or misunderstanding of this question, especially in the politically correct climate of America. But it's a fact that during the Spanish Inquisition, the Catholic Church and the Spanish government worked together to murder enormous numbers of people, perhaps millions. Nobody knows exactly how many people suffered and died by the most brutal methods ever devised by man. Some of these instruments of torture were designed to inflict agony for the longest periods of time while confessions were extracted. Their methods of torture and execution included the garotte, the wheel, hangings, beatings, burnings, drownings, and so on.

The physical results of this horrible age are still being experienced by souls who are incarnated today. Those tortures left their imprint on the energy patterns of many victims. These injustices will mark the aura because they haven't been balanced. Gerhard believes that if a person is executed because of actual wrongdoing, there's a karmic justice or balance. Crime and punishment. In other words, the punishment is accepted by the wrongdoer as fitting the crime.

On the other hand, if a person was unjustly executed or murdered, there is no karmic balance, and the pain is remembered and stored in the aura. In the Inquisition, for example, people were not executed for actual wrongdoing but were tortured and murdered to satisfy the demands of a criminal religious authority. These murders were the result of every evil impulse known to humanity having sway over the ones in power—religion and government, hand in hand, not showing any mercy in the infliction of pain and suffering on the hearts and minds and bodies of God's children. The karmic consequences of that orgy of torment are still being felt in the bodies of those who suffered and in the souls of those who inflicted that pain.

In a war, one could expect to be wounded or killed. In domestic turmoil and family tragedies, one might expect consequences from disastrous relationships and personal wrongs. The irony is that we are all God's children, even the ones inflicting the pain.

Torture and death come in many ways, and our bodies are afflicted accordingly. Down the ages, there have been so many injustices and horrors perpetrated that it is not the purpose of this book to detail every torture and possible effect on future lives. It is enough to say that the damage is actually felt at more than a physical level and the consequences may be experienced many hundreds of years later.

Some Examples of Past Life Injuries

Poison and Venom. More persons have died of snake and spider venom than by deliberately induced poison. Poison and venom may be stored and carried into the next life in the liver. An unreasonable fear of snakes and spiders might be a symptom of a lifetime ended in this way.

Hospitalization and Medical Experimentation. Dying in a hospital with tubes and needles in place or as a result of medical malpractice. The consequences of false medication would be the same as for poison. The Nazis performed many grisly experiments on human beings, including children. Most notably, Josef Mengele of Hitler's Third Reich conducted infamous medical experiments on twin children. Other Nazi tortures included freezing of concentration camp inmates.

Starvation. People have been starving ever since there were people. Even if starvation is not used as a tool of war or genocide, entire populations suffered from food shortages and famines. Millions were deliberately starved by the Nazis and also in Russia under the rule of Stalin just in the last century. In the next lifetime, it could be that a starvation victim might not ever be satisfied, eating to obesity.

As a side note, I wonder if America's high obesity rate might be due to millions of Holocaust victims seeking their next life in the Land of Plenty and finding the hunger to be insatiable. The result of this hunger in a past life could lead to a life where they can never eat enough.

Castration. To explain one consequence of castration, Gerhard has given us an example. The mother of a nine-year-old child named Willie came to Gerhard. The son had phimosis, which is a condition where the foreskin of the penis is too tight. He was also extremely shy. Gerhard asked Willie if he liked to sing. The mother interrupted without giving Willie a chance to answer and told Gerhard that the child had an unusual habit. When he was asked to sing a song in front of the classroom, he went to the teacher and stood beside him and would only sing in the teacher's ear. None of the other pupils were able to hear him.

Gerhard received a psychic impression that in an earlier life, Willie had a beautiful singing voice and had been castrated to preserve his boyish soprano, ostensibly to sing in the church choir or musical productions. As little as two hundred years ago, women in the Catholic Church were not allowed to sing in the church choir. In order to get soprano voices for the choir, little boys were often castrated. Thousands of little boys were castrated yearly in Italy and other European countries to meet this demand for sopranos. Many boys died as a result of infections caused by the castration. It is a historical fact that the famous composer, Joseph Haydn, because of his beautiful soprano voice, was to be castrated. However, his father was able to put a halt to this devilish plan before it could be carried out.

When the consciousness in this lifetime recalls this experience, it will attempt in every instance to avoid singing in public because there might be terrible consequences. The consciousness doesn't understand that nowadays, a beautiful singing voice willl not bring about castration. The boy will avoid singing alone at all costs. Singing in a choir will not result in individual attention to his singing talent. He will sing in the shower, he will sing at home, but he will have a problem in public. He will not want to draw attention to himself under any circumstances. Gerhard explained to Willie how it had happened and how it wouldn't happen again. This in conjunction with an aura healing helped Willie to release his fear of singing. He does have a nice singing voice.

This karmic pattern from earlier lifetimes will often cause prostate problems for men in later life.

Electric Chair. Klaus, an eleven-year-old boy with chronic tonsillitis, was brought by his mother to Gerhard. Gerhard detected a blockage in his neck and thought he would try to release it. He asked Klaus to seat himself in a chair and sat on his right side in another chair. As Gerhard began aura surgery on his neck, he observed something that appeared to be steam coming through the shirt from his left arm. Intuitively, Gerhard asked Klaus if he was afraid of electricity. Klaus's mother, who was standing next to him, answered for him. She said that Klaus refused to play with his brother's electric train set and was also afraid of every electrical appliance.

Next, Gerhard asked Klaus how he was doing in his English class. His mother answered that Klaus was in the second year of high school and had gotten very good grades in the first year. In this year, however, he was always getting poor grades. His teacher in the second year English class had spent a long time as a teacher in the United States and spoke American English.

From this information, Gerhard was shown a picture of an electric chair and wondered if Klaus carried in his unconsciousness a cell memory of an execution by this method and if the memory had been unlocked by hearing the teacher with the American accent. It would also explain his fear of electrical appliances. Gerhard then used his hands to feel the energy around his head and felt the energy of a copper plate. He told Klaus what he was feeling and then removed it. As he took it away from the aura, Klaus said he felt immediately lighter and more relaxed.

Upon questioning, Gerhard learned that Klaus would not wear a cap on his head, no matter how cold it was. Every time his head was touched in the slightest way, he was filled with fear and pain. After Gerhard took the copper plate out of his aura, he touched his head again. Klaus had no pain and no fear. Several weeks later, Klaus's mother called Gerhard and told him that Klaus was doing very well in English and he was getting good grades again. He's also able to wear his cap during the cold German winters.

15

Human Energy Systems Laboratory

Tucson, Arizona, July 2001

MY HUSBAND AND I moved to Arizona in 1999 after a twelve-year stay in Germany. In October 2000, Gerhard came for his first visit in Arizona. Without fully knowing how I would promote his healing, I was able to find audiences for him everywhere. I used the telephone book to contact bookstores, spiritualist churches, and New Age groups and even advertised a demonstration at the local Best Western hotel. An audience was found everywhere, and he was not disappointed with the reception provided by Tucson and Green Valley residents. Everyone he saw was impressed with his sincerity and his special gifts.

One morning in spring 2001, as I was getting dressed for work, a daytime talk show was on television, and I suddenly came to attention when I heard the words energy healing and aura. Professor Gary E. Schwartz was discussing his experiments with energy and healing at the University of Arizona. I was very excited when I heard that he was in Tucson, which is just a forty-five-minute drive away from our home in Green Valley. I knew that I had to bring these two together. Until that time, I had never heard about Gary or his research.

Gerhard was eager for science to research and validate what he saw in his healing. He knew that the "miracles" he witnessed deserved scientific attention and that with the right research methods, a natural explanation would be found. Intuitively and spiritually, he knew that he had a unique ability—but he also knew that answers could be found if it were only researched thoroughly by open-minded persons. He couldn't just accept it as a gift from God. His education and background required a scientific and rational understanding. This desire led him to ongoing experimentation with different techniques and methods, and he was totally unafraid of how it might look to others. He knew that he wanted an explanation of the process. He wanted answers. He's that serious about what he's doing.

I found that Dr. Schwartz was a professor of psychology, medicine, neurology, psychology, psychiatry, and surgery at the University of Arizona. He was currently directing a research program on energy healing at the Human Energy Systems Laboratory. I wondered why I had not been aware of this research before Gerhard came in 2000.

So, I e-mailed Professor Schwartz and told him about Gerhard and what he was doing. I received a prompt and positive response that he would indeed be interested in meeting Gerhard and that I should bring him around to his office for a conversation on his next trip. When I e-mailed Gerhard, he immediately booked a flight. On April 15, 2001 (my birthday!), we were seated in Gary's office on campus. I watched with excitement and satisfaction as they seemed to find an immediate rapport. As they began to discuss the philosophy of healing and the connection to a higher power or energy source, I watched them both and marveled at their earnestness, at their conviction, and most of all, at their commitment to understanding the process.

They found agreement on many of their conjectures as to the nature of energy healing. Gary invited Gerhard to perform a number of demonstrations and experiments and participate in his research. Gerhard readily agreed, and it wasn't very long before we began to meet a lot of people from the university and the university hospital that were interested in alternative medicine.

On July 18, 2001, Gerhard was scheduled to conduct a demonstration at the Human Energy Systems Laboratory at the University of Arizona under the guidance and direction of Gary Schwartz. This was a bit different from Gerhard's usual gathering. Up until this time, Gerhard's audience consisted of persons who were in search of healing or were interested in discovery of higher truths. This time, he was facing graduate students who were assisting Dr. Schwartz in his research. They were designing experiments for something that had never been seriously researched. Also present were some other healers, notably Reiki healers, who were interested in seeing what this healer from Germany was doing. It was a young group with different expectations. Some were quite prepared to see him as a huckster with a tool box. Doing surgery with instruments? Come on, now ... let's get real.

Gerhard offered a brief explanation of how he worked and how he had discovered his abilities. He then offered to demonstrate his techniques. He asked if anyone was interested in receiving a reading/healing. It seemed that everyone in the room wished to experience whatever it was that Gerhard was doing, and one by one, they took a seat in front of Gerhard while their fellow students took notes and asked questions. Dan, one of the graduate students, filmed each healing session. As each individual stood by Gerhard, the students and observers were almost all taking notes and asking questions. Gerhard is able to conduct a healing session and answer questions at the same time. Although he does need a relatively calm environment to work, each question and comment was welcomed and responses were given. Gerhard politely explained what he was feeling in the individual energy fields (auras) and responded to questions with thoughtful answers, or a simple response that he didn't know.

Since Gerhard's methods are so unconventional (even in this unconventional field), and because of his use of instruments and tools, some people are understandably incredulous when he opens his kit. Among other things, he commonly uses syringes, needles, scissors, and keys.

Some of the exclamations I heard were, "What are you feeling?"

"Close your eyes—don't look!"

"Look at the size of that needle!"

Gerhard is also a medium and believes that he is assisted by doctors from the spirit world who have teamed up to offer their help. His guides act as ushers or emcees. Gerhard understands that these physicians that have begun to support him from the other side have grown in their understanding and wish to be influential in guiding this type of healing on this side. His medical team is always present at the healings. Messages of a personal nature seldom come through at a healing session. It's as if the doctors want to maintain an impersonal connection. However, when one of them does happen to deliver a personal message for the client through Gerhard, it is always met with astonishment. These rare personal messages seem to be 100 percent correct and serve to validate the healing immediately.

Every one of the healings on this day was videotaped by the research team for later analysis. The researchers took notes and asked questions while Gerhard worked. All but one of the participants reported healing to some degree— some more than others, and two or three quite dramatic in nature. Each was given a follow-up questionnaire. We didn't have access to the questionnaires completed by the subjects, so we don't know what they reported, but my personal, unscientific observations that afternoon seemed to be consistent and positive. Gerhard's cure rate jumped off the scale. While he claimed an 82 percent success rate for his healings, this group was batting more than 90 percent! The consensus of the group after seven hours of continuous healing activity was that something was going on here!

Professor Schwartz wrapped up the session with a discourse on possible explanations for what was happening, including a conjecture as to whether it was a placebo effect.

Gerhard interposed that if it were of a placebo nature, it could save the health care system a lot of money if it were as effective as conventional surgery. For sure, it offered less of a risk to the patient. The worst scenario of Gerhard's treatment would be that it didn't help. The patient had no risk of a botched surgery, infection, wrong anesthesia, wrong medication, or mistaken diagnosis. It should be kept in mind that most people are seen and treated by physicians and specialists when they are ill. They only look into alternative methods when conventional medicine has already failed to diagnose and cure the problem.

For those whose health had been influenced by past life experiences, he found several persons who had been hanged, two or three slaves, a bullet, a spear, and some other miscellaneous psychic injuries in the aura.

I remember in particular a lady named Jo Ann and her husband. Someone told me that Jo Ann was a noted local medium. Her husband accompanied her to this demonstration as he had suffered with chronic headaches for the past six years. This day, he reported a total relief from pain for the first time in that time period. She also claimed to be helped by the experience.

Sabrina and Dan—what a couple! They're both sensitives of the first degree. She had allergies. Gerhard found mold in her aura and said that he saw a dark, damp place ... could be from past life, perhaps in a dungeon, or it could be from this life. Suddenly, the room was alive with comments and laughter. Gerhard had no way of knowing it, but Sabrina had formerly lived in an apartment on campus that was owned by the university. The apartment was located in a historic neighborhood, and the building had been condemned by the Department of Health precisely because of a dangerous mold problem.

The condemnation process had been a major issue on campus and received heavy coverage from the local media. This was Gerhard's first encounter of a mold problem in America, and he had to search for the right word to describe what he was seeing, but it happened that he was right on target.

Dan suffered from a number of physical problems that Gerhard was able to target and identify. What was so remarkable about Dan was his sensitivity to everything that Gerhard did. In order to keep from being influenced by watching Gerhard's hands and actions, and to satisfy himself as to Gerhard's abilities, he kept his eyes closed during most of his treatment so that he wouldn't be influenced by what he was seeing. His reactions to Gerhard's treatment were significant in that he could identify the motions that Gerhard made—even when they were being made—behind him. In addition, when Gerhard had to give an injection in the aura, Dan winced and showed response to the syringe and needles.

At one point, he yelped, "Whoa!" and grabbed at his shoulder. Gerhard had given an injection with his needle in the area of the liver, but Dan had apparently felt something happening just beneath the neck area. He reported that this treatment apparently opened up a flow of some kind. This flow continued for quite a while during and after the treatment. After his treatment, which was dramatic in its effectiveness, he went over to the video camera and took over the filming while a colleague was treated. In the meantime,

Dan kept complaining of a severe new pain, which persisted and became worse. Finally, he returned to the treatment chair, and Gerhard gave him additional surgery.

This surgery was quite complicated and unusual with Gerhard apparently removing (and splintering in the process) what felt to Dan like a small log. Quite a few additional slivers and shards were removed, with each one causing Dan a lot of distress.

Dan asked, "What was that?"

Gerhard responded simply, "I don't know. How did it feel?"

"Like a big piece of wood, splintering and breaking while it was being pulled out."

The end result was that Dan was finally free of pain, but he was perplexed and astonished at his treatment. At the end of the session, he was totally pain free. I was privately wondering if he had been a victim of the notorious Vlad the Impaler! (Vlad was a mid-fifteenth century ruler of an empire in modern-day Romania who is estimated to have killed tens of thousands of his enemies by impaling them and watching them suffer a slow and painful death.)

Gary announced that it looked very hopeful that the laboratory would be able to fund his research with a grant from a private foundation.

It was arranged for Gerhard to appear at the laboratory the next day for some experiments with Kirlian photography.

The Kirlian Experiments

July 19, 2001. Again, Dan and Sabrina were present. She was to be the test subject for the Kirlian experiment. This time, the experiment would be conducted in the Human Energy Systems Laboratory, which appeared to be an odd hut that had but one very heavy door and no windows at all. The interior was very dark and oddly furnished—a long table with a computer monitor, a couple of office chairs, the camera equipment, and several more long tables with at least a dozen computer monitors lined up.

Dan told us that this laboratory was very special in that no energy could enter except what entered with us. No television signals, cell phone signals, or radio waves of any kind could enter or leave the building.

Before we began, though, Sabrina wanted us to see Dan's shoulder. She had noticed it that morning when Dan stepped out of the shower and was toweling off. There were about eight or ten perfectly round red spots on his shoulder, arranged in a very symmetrical manner, almost as if he had been burned through a grid of some kind. Dan said the spots didn't cause him any discomfort and indeed wouldn't have even noticed them if he'd lived alone. We used our digital camera to photograph the spots, which everyone could clearly see (except Dan).

Gerhard shrugged his shoulders. "It happens sometimes that there are spots or marks on treated areas."

Dan explained to Gerhard how the equipment worked and how measurements were made. A photographic film would be placed on top of a conducting plate and another conductor would be placed on the subject's thumb. The conductors would then be energized by a high-voltage power source and produce a photographic image to show a silhouette of the energy pattern for the subject surrounded by an aura of light.

As it would not be possible to photograph the aura during the healing itself because Gerhard needed both hands free to feel the aura, a decision was made to measure the energy fields of the healer and the subject before the healing began. About midway through the session, it would be halted for another Kirlian photograph of both persons, and then a final measurement taken when the healing session was completed. Dan was in charge of the equipment and monitor. Kirlian images were made for both Sabrina and Gerhard before the healing began. The images were not shown to Gerhard or to Sabrina at this time

A video camera was installed about six feet away from the healer and the subject. The healing would also be videotaped.

Gerhard began by raising both arms high over Sabrina's head and bringing them slowly down in a triangular pattern As he reached about the level of her ears, he stopped and announced that he had found a helmet in the aura. His interpretation was that death had occurred by a blow or injury to the head while wearing the helmet. The helmet and the damage were still present in the energy field. When he gave Sabrina that information, she told Gerhard that she had suffered from headaches of an unknown origin for her entire life and that no medical treatment or medication could relieve her pain. In fact, she came to the healing with a headache. Gerhard nodded in satisfaction, then set to work. He surgically removed the energy of the helmet from Sabrina and treated the deep head wound, which was still open. He then formed an energy pattern for the missing skull part. He closed the energy field. During the surgery, the headache completely disappeared and did not return for the duration of the healing.

When she announced that she felt better and Gerhard could no longer feel the blockage, he again started the testing pattern. He stopped at the middle of her back, where he had to remove a spear. Again, a warrior's death had been suffered by this young female college student. It was true that she also suffered from back pain more frequently than normal for a person her age. This too had to be treated.

Before Gerhard could go any further, Dan called a halt to the healing process and repeated the Kirlian photography on both subjects. Again, nothing was shown to Gerhard or Sabrina.

When they continued, Gerhard found damage to Sabrina's left leg at knee height. There was no energy for a kneecap, leaving a gap for energy flow. Again, she verified circulation problems in the left leg, for which there was no known reason. Gerhard treated this by opening the energy at the kneecap and cleaning it. He then injected liquid in the opening and closed it again.

After one more condition was cleared, he announced he was finished. Sabrina was very excited and reported that she felt she had received an amazing healing.

It was time to take the third set of Kirlian images, and then after a fifteen-minute wait, a fourth set of images were taken.

Dan then showed us the images in the sequence in which they were taken. The first image of Sabrina showed major energy gaps at the upper left portion of her head, two more gaps in the midsection of the torso, and no energy at all from the knee down on the left side! The entire energy pattern was filled with spurts and gaps. Gerhard's images, on the other hand, were very clean. Only tiny bits of energy seemed to be emanating from him, with the notable exception of a very large spurt of energy from the center of his head. The right arm had no energy at all from the shoulder to the elbow. Gerhard explained that he meditates before a healing session and he thinks his energy is very clean and neutral. It would make him a better channel if he wasn't broadcasting his own energy, so that explanation made perfect sense to me.

I wondered at the absence of any energy at all from Gerhard's right arm.

He laughed. "Do you remember my encounter with the jumping cholla last weekend?"

Gerhard is an avid photographer and had photographed a beautiful, blooming cholla, which repaid him with some needles in the upper arm, causing a lot of discomfort.

The second set of photos, taken during a break in the healing, now showed the energy pattern on the left side of Sabrina's head to be covered by a rectangular block of energy, which seemed to be more closed than the rays from the rest of the body. There was another block, which was very solid and much different from the energy patterns emanating from the rest of her body. Gerhard's energy is a bit more pronounced now, but still much less than that of Sabrina's. The large emanations from the top of the head are still more pronounced.

The healing continued. Gerhard found some other issues, explained them, and cleared them up, with Sabrina feeling better with every motion he made. He then announced that he was finished. Again, the Kirlian images were taken for the third time, and fifteen minutes later for a fourth time, and then fifteen minutes later for a fifth time. On Images Three, Four, and Five, Sabrina's energy was now uniform and glowing from head to toe, with no gaps whatsoever. It was beautiful! She was literally bathed in energy. The images reminded me immediately of paintings of the Madonna or holy figures, surrounded by a halo of energy or light.

Gerhard's images have also changed. His energy seemed to be uneven and spurting in every direction. The large energy pattern on top of his head was still extended out very far, but had closed upon itself, like a flaming halo. Images Four and Five for Gerhard showed an energy pattern that seemed to be settling down to a fuller pattern, but both of these images showed the major spurt at the head level, like a large arc over his head.

So, what did it all mean? Everything I've written above are my personal observations, and I'm not a scientist. Dr.

Schwartz was not present at this experiment, so we don't know what he made of it.

I know what Sabrina thought. She was happy and pain free. She wondered if Gerhard had time in the next few days to make an appointment for her mother to receive a healing from him. She knew what had happened.

Dan wanted to conduct another Kirlian experiment with Gerhard and was trying to think of something meaningful. While he was thinking, I jumped in with a suggestion.

Gerhard is able to remove earthbound entities from a person's aura. These entities are sometimes drawn into our energy fields, where they linger and cause headaches, depression, anxiety, and back and shoulder pain. The victim of these beings is actually carrying them around with all their problems. I wondered if the energies could be captured, how they would appear before and after they were released, or if they could be captured at all.

Both Dan and Gerhard were enthusiastic and thought it would be an interesting experiment. Dan decided to introduce a new element into the experiment. He explained that it was possible to filter the physical energies to produce only spiritual energies.

Dan made a set of images, filtered and unfiltered, for Gerhard before he invited the entity to come into his aura. Gerhad then entered into a brief meditation and announced that he had an entity with him. Dan then made a second set of images of Gerhard with his entity. Gerhard then released the entity, and a third set of images were produced.

Gerhard's energy field was dramatically larger and stronger in the second set of images (with the entity) and then back to normal in the third set (after it was released).

They decided to repeat this experiment. Gerhard opened himself up to another entity, but none came. He tried again but with no success. Gerhard was puzzled because he had never failed to find an earthbound entity before. Dan then remembered that it wasn't possible for new energy to come into the laboratory. The one we had found the first time must have come in with us. I never cease to be amazed at how this works.

The door was opened and we chatted a while. The door was again closed, and Gerhard tried again.

"I have one," he said calmly.

The experiment was repeated with the same result of the excessive energy gathering at the front of Gerhard's head during the time of the entity's presence.

It could be that this was the first time that earthbound entities have been captured and measured. Maybe capture is the wrong word. They volunteered.

So ended the Kirlian experiments. I don't know what Dr. Schwartz made of them, but it was very interesting for us. As a souvenir, Dan gave us a CD with all the images, which I was able to print out with my notes.

Demonstrations

During this time, more doctors and researchers from the University had heard about Gerhard, and we received many requests for demonstrations and healings. These were held in private homes with many persons in attendance. Gerhard gladly accepted every invitation and gave freely of his time and abilities. We met some very interesting people during this time, and some of the experiences are related elsewhere in this book.

One of the individuals we encountered was Dr. Iris Bell, professor of psychiatry and psychology. Dr. Bell is the director of research for the Center for Integrative Medicine at the University of Arizona College of Medicine. She is very interested in all healing, especially homeopathic medicine.

The common link, of course, is transformation and healing brought about by direction of energy.

Gerhard performed his aura surgeries. He removed earthbound entities. He delivered messages from departed relatives. He was thrilled to be able to meet and exchange ideas with physicians, naturopaths, homeopaths, psychic mediums, Reiki healers, spiritualist ministers, professionals, socialites, and working people.

One Sunday afternoon at the home of a University professor, twenty or thirty persons had gathered to meet Gerhard and learn about his methods and healing experiences. Gerhard demonstrated his aura surgery on almost every guest. These were not private sessions; it seemed that everyone wanted to see what he did with everyone else. There were a lot of questions, and Gerhard shared his ideas and techniques freely with all who were present. The questions were unusual in that they involved highly technical issues and procedures. While Gerhard was working, someone told me that most of the guests were doctors and other professionals from the University Medical Center. We were very impressed and gratified by how open many professionals were to this type of treatment.

When it seemed that everyone there had experienced a healing, someone asked if Gerhard could heal the large dog who had been present all evening. He had been taken to the vet just the day before for some sort of ailment but was now seated in the middle of the living room, looking at all the guests and eager for interaction with someone.

Gerhard was a bit puzzled as to how to go about healing the dog. He protested that he'd never tried to heal an animal before. It was a convivial group, however, and he agreed to give it a try. I happened to be seated on the sofa at the time, and the dog was watching me and asking for my attention. (I had been petting him a lot.)

Gerhard moved behind the dog, raised his hands, and

tried to feel the dog's aura. The dog ignored him, still looking at me, but Gerhard was apparently satisfied that he'd found something to be treated and opened a new syringe to give the dog some spiritual medication. As he inserted the needle into the dog's aura (around the right haunch), the dog suddenly wheeled around and tried to nip Gerhard.

He had felt the syringe, even though it was half an inch away from his skin! The dog's reaction was impressive, proving the point that this was no placebo effect. The dog certainly had not anticipated or understood that he was being healed, but he had felt the presence of the needle and reacted defensively!

Feedback

During the course of Gerhard's stay, a questionnaire and consent form was handed to each one of his clients that agreed to participate in the study at the University of Arizona. We do not know which of the contacts returned the consent forms, the content of any returned forms, or how they were tabulated. Dozens of people did agree to take part in the study and share personal information with the researchers and students. We carefully observed the rules of confidentiality and handed out forms to Gerhard's clients at the end of each healing session and workshop held during a three-week period in July 2001.

The feedback we personally received was quite good, and most persons seemed improved or healed. Gerhard was fully booked during this time because so many people were telling their friends about their results. Many people had to be turned away for lack of time. All that is anecdotal and unscientific, however, and Gerhard yearned for validation from science. (Recall his patent office experience!)

Dr. Schwartz eventually published his book, *The Energy Healing Experiments*, in 2008. The book was positive on the entire subject of energy healing. Gerhard returned to Europe and continued to explore his talents, help people where he could, and seek scientists to clarify and explain his unique talent. He's succeeded in every respect and continues to cooperate with scientists and medical professionals in every way. He very much hoped for validation and explanation of his abilities, but it was not to happen at that time. He is still eager to cooperate with any scientific experiment that may offer clues to this healing process and believes that the field of quantum physics will eventually provide an explanation for the effectiveness of aura surgery.

Gerhard has received every confirmation and validation that he needs to know that he is on the correct path and that his life is exactly on target with a plan, even though he may not always see the exact direction. He knows he will never retire and that he is extremely blessed and loved.

16

Orbs, Globes, and Fireflies

DURING GERHARD'S VISIT IN July and August 2002, a new phenomenon emerged for us. I'm a night owl, working at my computer or reading until the wee hours of the morning. Normally, I'm quiet, not wanting to disturb others in the house. However, on Monday, July 29, I was listening to the Art Bell Show, which is broadcast from coast to coast in the middle of the night. This evening, the show centered on an aspect of photography that seemed to be a psychic manifestation, producing orbs and globes. People traveled to cemeteries, haunted houses, and battle-fields to produce pictures of floating orbs and globes and sometimes an amorphous form floating over the landscape. Intrigued, I thought of my own digital camera that I use for real estate photos, and I thought of the psychic healer sound asleep in the guest bedroom. The next day, I called several friends, and that evening, we gathered in the living room to conduct a healing and experimental photogra-phy session. This time, the healing and group meditation would be recorded with two cameras. One was a normal 35 mm automatic focus Olympus camera and the other was a Sony Mavica FP73, which records digital images to a floppy disk. The Sony Mavica is a digital camera that I used at that time to take pictures of houses, living rooms, gardens, and mountain views. I'd used that camera for over a year, and nothing unusual had ever occurred in my photographs. I considered it a great asset for a real estate broker.

Something very special, however, happened that evening. There were only five people present: Gerhard, Justin, Trisha, Abby, and me. We all knew that the evening was to be a spontaneous experiment in a totally uncontrolled and unscientific environment (the living room). We discussed that we hoped to photograph Gerhard's spirit doctors or his spirit guides, perhaps even the earthbound entities who sometimes came to Gerhard to be freed and sent home. If nothing else happened, we enjoyed being with one another and welcomed the opportunity to spend an evening with Gerhard and his remarkable abilities.

We began the evening with a guided meditation from Gerhard. The Ave Maria played softly on the stereo, and candles were lit to put us in the proper mood. The meditation ended, and then I added a special invitation to the spirit world to cooperate and consent with this experiment if it were possible and desirable for us to experience it. Gerhard began by blessing a chair and preparing a place for his spirit guide. Photos of the chair were taken before, during, and after the blessing. Both cameras were flashing—Justin on the 35 mm and me with my digital camera. I noticed immediately that something wasn't right.

The photos of the chair blessings were very interesting in that the first photo was normal—clear and no orbs or anything unusual happening. The next photo was out of focus and cloudy except for a bright little orb that seemed to soak up all the light. It was hovering over the chair that was being blessed.

Fig. 3. Chair before blessing.

Fig. 4. Chair being blessed and "occupied"

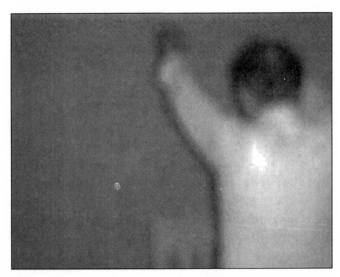

Since that camera had an automatic focus and the flash functioned properly, it was puzzling. I wondered if it was because I was taking the pictures more rapidly than I normally did with my real estate photos. I slowed down and gave the lens and flash time to recover. Same result. This had never happened before. The flash was bright, and the exposure was correct, but the picture was totally blurred with tiny flashes of light on the screen. This was an unexpected development.

The next few pictures looked good on the display screen, so I continued to snap slowly and methodically, but it was still occasionally going totally out of focus. I couldn't make it blur by moving the camera quickly—some pictures were in focus, and some were not. Just looking at the display screen didn't provide any explanation. I clicked on, one picture after another, until the floppy disk was full. I replaced it and continued without looking at the pictures on the computer screen.

Gerhard asked if anyone needed a healing, and Trisha volunteered that she had been having trouble with her foot. The photography continued, but it was necessary to give more light to the healer, thus changing the lighting conditions in the room. After that healing, Abby requested help, and Gerhard continued his healing with her. The cameras flashed, and disks were filled. Justin needed more film, and that camera was reloaded.

Trisha then asked if Gerhard could help her with a jaw or tooth problem. He said he would try, but the lights had to go up even higher for this kind of close surgery. We continued with our photography. Gerhard is able to work under the most public conditions, and it's very hard to shake his concentration while he's healing.

At some point during the photography, I suddenly noticed something on the display screen that definitely wasn't visible in the room. When the camera flashed, I saw an egg-shaped object that seemed to be glowing. Justin and Abby gathered around my camera, and we all saw that I'd photographed something unusual. I continued to take more shots until the healing was completed. At that point, we couldn't wait any longer, and we took the disks to a computer and looked at what we'd photographed. Stunned, we watched as image after image flashed on the monitor. Almost every picture contained an anomaly! The pictures showed colorful orbs, transparent globes, and twinkling fireflies. The bright little fireflies seemed to catch the camera's focus and produce totally blurred images. Some photos contained most unusual, filmy white mists that almost obscured the entire room. Occasionally, a perfectly normal picture with no orbs or anomalies surfaced, as if to say, "See, it's not the camera!"

They were almost all unusual, but most striking of all was a sequence of photos during Trisha's jaw surgery. The first unusual photo showed Trisha getting ready to take a seat in front of Gerhard, who was already seated in a dining room chair. Gerhard was looking at his instruments, which were spread out neatly on a white towel on a table at his right hand. Hovering about seven or eight inches above the instruments was a beautiful orb of a bluish color. The top left edge of the orb had a red-orange glow, and the bottom right appeared to have small energy flares. The energy flares looked like those depicted in Kirlian photography. In the photo, both Gerhard and the orb seemed to have a waiting attitude. (It's entirely possible that our imaginations were transferring this attitude into the picture!) It was truly amazing to see. We didn't know what we wanted when we began, but were stunned at what we actually got. It was a bit overwhelming to absorb. We certainly hadn't expected this kind of success.

Three shots later, from almost the same angle, after the surgery had begun, the orb appeared again, this time a bit

something interesting was planned? Most important to us, did they appear in our photos by chance or design?

Lastly and most puzzling, why had I never photographed anything like this in my life before the night we asked for spirit photos? This was too much of a coincidence for anyone to believe!

A few days after our orb experiment, and while we were still puzzling about it, Gerhard was invited for a television interview on Access Tucson, a local public television station. The interview went well, and we started home after we'd enjoyed a cup of coffee at the Hotel Congress across the street from the television station. While we were driving, I received a telephone call from a lady who had seen the program and wanted an appointment with Gerhard as soon as possible.

I asked her, "What in the program impressed you to call for an immediate appointment?"

She replied, "I'm a psychic medium, and I could see the spirits hovering around him. That's how I know that he is also a true medium."

"How do they appear to you?" I asked.

"They look like orbs and globes. I see them all the time."

Gerhard was completely booked for the next week, but I invited her for an evening with us because I was curious about the orbs. She agreed, and we had a fascinating evening. Her insights were very interesting.

Asking a Clairvoyant about the Orbs and Globes

Nicole is a charming young lady who lives in Tucson and is a successful and talented medium and clairvoyant. This is what she says about the orbs and globes:

The big balls like that are actually going to be persons or animals that have been connected to the earth and are now earthbound. The smaller ones that would be nickel and dime size—very bright and very piercing—those have intelligence. There are a multitude of ranges of intelligence. There's intelligence that is attached to the earth's development and will play a role in what we're doing—in our spiritual development and our consciousness and our awareness.

There are dimensions of intelligence that don't seem to be interested in us or our agenda. They sort of roam around, pop in and out, exploring the universe. Most of the other dimensions can see us, but we're not as entertaining as we like to think we are. I think the blue lights are people's guides, your direct guide system. Those are the ones that I've found, through my own observations, with sitting with people. The clear little ones, like when I'm in a reading, will download me information, like in paragraph form.

The fireflies sometimes arrange themselves in a constellation effect. They pass me information in a big glob of understanding. It then takes me about fifteen minutes to go through all that and pass it on to the subject of the reading. I think that the really, really big ones with different colored lights and patterns inside are angels!

While she was visiting with us, Nicole remarked on a strong floral smell that she felt was either an angel or a divine mother.

Gerhard asked Nicole if she thought anything we photographed might be ascended masters. She said she believed they were always present, but if you raised the vibration, like bringing in sound, you opened your third eye, and you would have a lot of smaller ones show up. The brighter ones were the stronger force.

Nicole said it was important to note the different kinds of orbs we got with different folks in different settings.

She said, "The living room environment, for example, or home, will have more of the clear and translucent orbs. When you add sound to your environment, you'll get more of the little bright ones, who go whooshing in and out, and you feel like they're talking to you, like they're paying attention."

I wish to add that a little bright orb seems most interested in Gerhard's healing and especially his instruments. We have many photographs taken at healings that show an orb hovering over the instruments. We have several photos showing an orb hovering over the closed bag.

Scientists dispute the appearance of these orbs—even scientists who claim to be open-minded about spiritual healing dislike accepting evidence from orb photography. We just think it interesting that they seem to always be present during healings and other spiritual activity.

On one occasion, we went to a spiritualist church for a meditation session. The digital camera was used discreetly in the back of the room to photograph the proceedings. Over two hundred photos were taken with no orbs or unusual effects—until Gerhard began a healing with music demonstration. Then, several bright little orbs appeared to hover at the back or shoulder area of the person receiving the healing. One orb even appeared to be waiting in line, moving up through several frames and then appearing at the back of the neck of the person it was following when it was that person's turn to be healed.

This particular orb was very interesting to me because it seemed to be moving up in line, following a young man. As he came to the front of the line, it suddenly appeared onto the back of his neck. The photograph was remarkable, and I showed it to Gerhard. He agreed that it was peculiar and he felt that the orb might be helping to open the throat chakra and facilitate the healing.

We were both so excited about these photos, which appeared to show actual intent and involvement in human affairs. I wanted to make sure that I didn't lose them, so I copied them to another disk and then to my hard drive. It was very late, so we retired for the evening. The next day, I looked for the photos to show my husband, and they were nowhere to be found. These were the only photos that I have actually lost. I've deleted lots on purpose, but these were the only ones that I'd accidentally deleted.

I actually handed the disks to a computer expert at Raytheon to try to recover the photos, but he had no luck. I regret the loss of those photos very much.

Another interesting orb appeared during a workshop when Gerhard was going from one participant to another and touching into their auras. He gave quick personal readings on their energy. As he approached one young man and felt his energy, Gerhard announced, "I'm sensing the vibration of the Mother Mary with you." He was known to the other participants to be Jewish, so that was an interesting observation by Gerhard.

The young man smiled and said, "She was a good Jewish girl."

I was present at this workshop and was taking photographs. The first photo showed Gerhard taking the man's hand to pull him out of the circle and was not remarkable. The next shot showed Gerhard and the man, and at the young man's left shoulder there was a beautiful glowing aqua orb. The color was beautiful and vibrant. Of the thousands of photos I have taken, before and after this workshop, not one photo showed an orb of that color and brilliance. When I questioned Gerhard later, he said that he had experienced this vibration in a few other readings, so it was not unique for him, but it was unusual..

Some scientists and experts claim that the orbs and globes are anomalies created by the digital camera. I can state unequivocally that I never had a single orb from my digital camera until we asked a higher source to provide evidence. I asked for them. If this were just a camera anomaly, I should have had one or two orbs prior to our experimentation. I was a real estate agent at this time, and it was routine for me to take up to 100 pictures at one time of exteriors, interiors, garages and gardens. All the indoor pictures utilized a flash. I would choose the best for my ads and flyers. Until this evening, I had no orbs and globes flying through my real estate photos.

For a while, I collected orb photos like a fanatic. I photographed in cemeteries, houses where I knew people had passed away, churches, homes, parks, my patio, and anywhere else I thought might produce orbs. I went out into the rain and made photos with lots of orbs created by the moisture droplets... these are consistent and explainable.

I went to an accident site where several young people had died and photographed a most disturbing red energy that appeared to have a dog face, not unlike that of Sirius, an Egyptian deity. It hung very high in the night sky over the crash scene, which had been covered with flowers and mementos.

Some orbs really are reflections of pollen or dust. I shook a dust mop and photographed the hundreds of orbs that resulted. They were entirely different.

I spent an amazing evening at a cemetery in Salisbury, North Carolina, where thousands of Union prisoners of war had been buried in a mass trench. This prison was liberated and burned in 1865 in the closing days of the Civil War. I was visiting a friend in Salisbury and prevailed upon her to drive me to the cemetery at dusk. I photographed an incredibly bright energy hovering at an old grave with fresh flowers. I photographed another orb bopping along between the gravestones, and its progress could be marked over several photos by using a waste can as an indicator. It was in Salisbury that I saw something very high in the sky on one of the photos. It was green and only a bit of imagination was required to announce that it was an angel!

My living room, which is not dust free, normally has no orb activity; however, any meditation session or spiritual music and meditation will bring them in to be photographed. Our experience has led us to determine that it has everything to do with intention. If it is your intention and desire to produce orb photos, you have a very good chance of being successful. I certainly didn't have any before we made a decision to experiment with our digital cameras.

Two amazing photographs emerged from this era. One photo was of Gerhard at the dining room table, working at his laptop. I was happily snapping away with my digital camera and aimed the camera at him. We were astonished to see a large tubular shape with a gassy appearance materializing or moving on the right side of the photo.

The other was taken at a nighttime re-enactment at the Presidio San Agustin del Tucson, a historic location in downtown Tucson. Volunteers were dressed in period clothing to depict soldiers from the days of the Spanish occupation. Uniformed soliders were drilling and firing cannons. I got quite a few orbs, one picture of something emerging from the ground, and an amazing photo of orbs and streaks of light. My impression of the light streaks was that a regiment of soldiers had just ridden through the encampment. The pictures before and after were fairly normal photos. The streaks of light were bright orange. Accompanying them were dozens of standard translucent orbs. Strange.

Orb photography became my passion after Gerhard returned home to Germany. When I was finally satisfied that many (not all) orbs were an indicator of spiritual activity, I returned to using my digital camera for family holidays, real estate activity, and vacations. I am now mostly orb free in my photographs but have no doubt that they will return again if they are invited.

At first, the orb photography seemed like a diversion from the healing and only meant new puzzles. Gerhard was interested in the occurrence, but not as involved as I in the experimentation. His primary goal has always been healing and this was an interesting side show for him that never distracted him from his healing pursuits.

We both viewed the orb activity as confirmation of the guidance and intelligence behind the healings. This was very important to observe the types of orbs which appeared when Gerhard was sensing the presence of earth-bound entities. Nicole provided us her insights into the phenomenon, and it was more than a coincidence that she telephoned for an appointment after she saw Gerhard on television. She was able to speak to the subject from her personal experience and viewpoint.

Meeting Hans Holzer

In August 2002, Gerhard was again back in Arizona. He had run across a copy of the book *Beyond Medicine Healing* by Hans Holzer, a well-known pioneer in parapsychology and the author of over one hundred books on hauntings and paranormal events. The book resonated so much with him that he would not rest until he had met Dr. Holzer.

Dr. Holzer wrote, "If good health is the norm of the body, and medical treatment can effect no improvement, then the reason for the illness must be looked for in other areas, such as karmic preconditions, failure to understand self or to live in harmony with self, or psychic incursions."

This was exactly Gerhard's philosophy, and he wanted to speak with him personally and discuss healing at length with this distinguished author and researcher.

We called Dr. Holzer's publisher and were able to speak with him by telephone. Within forty-eight hours, Gerhard was on his way to New York! He stayed in Hans's apartment for four days, and they talked about everything—everything! They spent a great deal of time talking about healing and the philosophy of healing.

They had so much in common and so much to share. Gerhard showed Hans the orb photos and asked his opinion. Hans had heard about this phenomena but had not studied them. He did, however, put forth a theory that the digital camera doesn't have its own consciousness and stores the images as balls of light that we call orbs.

A side note to this visit with Hans Holzer is that Gerhard saw a large autographed photo of Hans Adam II, Prince of Liechtenstein, in Hans's library. Hans told Gerhard that he knew the prince very well. Gerhard had never met this gentleman, but it was the only photograph among dozens that he inquired about. The very next year, Gerhard received permission to acquire a permanent residence in Liechtenstein! Probably just a coincidence.

Psychics and children are sometimes able to see spirit forms and faces that are not visible to most of us. If a spirit is present in a room, a psychic would say that a being was present and describe details in its appearance. The camera would record a ball of light or streak, perhaps in motion. The camera interprets information in one way, and a psychic will interpret the information in an entirely different way.

Consciousness seems to be an important part of orb photography. My husband has no interest in paranormal activity, so we prevailed upon him to try to capture orbs with the same camera and under the same conditions. He filled up a floppy disk on that first orb night and captured no orbs at all!

We have continued our research into orbs, and some really surprising and interesting photos have been taken. We still discuss what it all means, and a conclusion is nowhere in sight. We have tried to produce orbs and have some great fake orb photos produced by dust, insects, hairs, and moisture droplets. There is a noticeable difference in the orbs we produce on purpose and the ones that occur by chance.

17

Power of Love

Someday, after mastering the winds, the waves, the tides and gravity, we shall harness for God the energies of love, and then, for a second time in the history of the world, man will have discovered fire.

—Pierre Teilhard de Chardin

ONE OF THE FIRST lessons learned by psychologists, advertising executives, business consultants, and educators is that people are more highly motivated by reward and recognition than by fear and punishment. Only a free society creates the best environment for evolution of the human soul. Therefore, the teachings of the churches as they relate to punishment and fear of purgatory or eternal damnation are no longer valid or relevant. The human soul cannot evolve in the presence of fear and hatred.

By living in a material world, we can scarcely recognize our own truths, our own reality. When we listen to a gifted speaker, politician, or minister, we are led to believe in a reality which may not be our truth. So often, the new reality that we accept is only an illusion created by others for the purpose of gaining control and authority over us. The problem with this, however, is that if we hear a mantra again and again, we will eventually accept it as a truth, without any examination or proof. We must experience our own truths.

Only the person who lives with a conscious awareness of his ties with the infinite spirit will find enlightenment and thus freedom. That freedom involves taking conscious responsibilities for all of his thoughts and actions.

This is only possible if we recognize and acknowledge that the goal of our lives is the restoration of full unity with God. The fulfillment of God's love—and thus, in the first place, of love to ourselves—because we consist of body, mind, and soul. Self-love includes love of the physical body as well as attention to the spiritual aspects of one's being. A love that consists only of a spiritual love in this material world is not a complete love. A love that is only concerned with the physical side of a relationship is also not a complete love.

The person who neglects his health or abuses the body with reckless behavior cannot be living in full conscious awareness and will not have a complete relationship with God.

I Love, Therefore I Am

The Christian churches of today have still not succeeded in achieving the desired result of living in accordance with the ideals of Christianity.

George Bernard Shaw stated, "**Christianity** might be a good thing if anyone ever tried it." Fear of freedom and fear of joy are the result of centuries of religious indoctrination, which creates fear. Power rests solely in the hands of religious authority.

Jesus said in John 14:12 (King James version): "Verily, verily, I say unto you, He that believeth on me, the works that I do shall he do also; and greater works than these shall he do; because I go unto my Father."

St. Augustine of Hippo: "Miracles are not contrary to nature but only contrary to what we know about nature."

The internal concentration and focus on God as the epitome of love, goodness and perfect and infinite Spirit has healing and restorative effect. Thus, healing cannot be separated from love. Disease is a cry for help coming from the body; it is simply a lack of love.

One of the primary forgotten doctrines of Christianity is that we face life with joy. Most of the hymns, however, speak of earthly life as a vale of tears, sorrow, and strife, with the reward to come in the hereafter. Only then can we walk on the streets of gold.

The teachings of Jesus are of a thoroughly positive nature. Jesus never spoke of negatives, and he never imposed a judgment. His words and deeds were expressions of pure and boundless love for all creatures.

The teachings of Jesus have nothing to do with solemn pomp and ritual formality, since this precludes any spontaneity of expression and joy. Are we to believe that Jesus never laughed or shared a joke with his friends and family? He grew up in a Jewish land, and the Jewish people are well known for their humor and love of jokes.

We must learn to laugh more and to spread joy. We develop our personality when we believe in our divine mission and share it with others without preaching or coercion. Only then are we able to develop a free and liberated sense of being.

Darwin believed that the loss of the sense of the artistic results in a loss of happiness, which is harmful to the mind.

Random Thoughts

Make time for periods of silence. Nature is doing the same as winter in a time of silence.

Relax at a mental and physical level. There is a time to be lazy.

Use your imagination. See the beauty that is in everything.

Trust in your own experiences and beliefs and not those imposed by others.

Open to the truth and the pursuit of truth through reading and music

Self-determination has nothing to do with egotism but is the recognition that we are at one with God.

A habit can only be changed when we turn our attention elsewhere. If we are to overcome evil in the world, we do not achieve it with constant warfare and by personification of the devil in the form of Satan. We must strengthen the good. We need our faith directed toward the good by actively resisting evil.

Many people are afraid to use the word love, feel guilty if they feel love for another human being, and are ashamed to show love openly. Love is life; it is not an abstract emotion. If someone is filled with love, he radiates light and joy, which are reflected by others. Thus, love comes back to the originator.

In the same way, however, negative judgments, hatred, and jealousy will also return to the originator and strengthen its negative effects. Negative judgments on other persons serve only to reinforce and strengthen the pride and ego of the one who judges others. Jesus said, "Judge not that ye be not judged."

Where is the true faith of people and churches when they speak of eternal damnation? How can anyone see God in this way? In particular, the power that people have conferred upon their churches to judge and declare which sins are punishable by eternal suffering with no relief or forgiveness.

This is evidence only of a lack of love and faith in God. Love is the only force that multiplies by division. By giving love unconditionally, you are in a position to receive love unconditionally. If the heart is considered to be a symbol of love, is heart disease a symptom of a lack of love? Just a question.

Love has a magnetic attraction. If we love ourselves, we will attract like-minded persons, and we will receive love in the same manner we give love.

The only real freedom in the world for all people, regardless of where they come from, is freedom of thought.

We are free if we recognize the truth in everything we see without the necessity of intellectual analysis and confirmation.

Only human beings can deprive themselves of the freedom God gave them. Only we have the free will to accept freedom or choose slavery of the ego.

It is all very well and good if we admire others because of

their appearance, talent, or skills, but we should be aware that every person possesses an admirable quality, even though it might not be immediately visible. For me, it is clear that each person has been given by God everything that he or she needs to make his or her way in this world. Envy of the abilities of others or blind imitation of others will hinder the development and growth of our own potential. Every person is unique and perfect in its own creation.

Happiness is neither moral nor immoral. Happiness is a state of mind. Happiness is a God-given right. If we do not accept this gift from God, or we don't make use of this gift, it will be as if it never existed.

A person can only be happy when he lives in harmony with nature.

If, however, we only expect happiness in the future, and not in the present, we are not in harmony with the happiness that is possible for us now. If we only see obstacles and blocks to overcome, we are missing out on today's potential.

If we understand that the only things in the world that we can successfully improve are ourselves and our fellow human beings, then we will stop tilting at windmills.

That makes it even more important to avoid prejudice of any kind. Attitudes can only change if we are liberated from prejudice.

18

Areas of Future Study

By Gerhard Kluegl

There is no matter in itself. All matter only occurs and exists through a force that starts the atomic particles vibrating and holds them together as the tiniest solar system of the atom. But since, in the whole universe, there is neither an intelligent nor an eternal force, we must assume that there is a conscious, intelligent spirit behind this force. This spirit is the very basis of all matter.

It is not the visible and transient matter that is real, absolute, true—because, as we have seen, matter could not exist at all without this spirit; it is the invisible, immortal spirit that is true.

But since spirit cannot exist on its own, because every spirit belongs to a being, we have to accept the concept of a spiritual being. But since even spiritual beings cannot come into existence on their own, but have to be created, I do not shy from naming this mysterious creator just as other cultured peoples of the earth in earlier centuries called him: GOD.

—Max Planck, from a lecture given in the Harnack House in 1929 (unpublished manuscript)

A Holistic Approach to Health Maintenance and Cures

One of the advantages of a holistic approach to health is the active creation of conditions for the next body. One of the goals of this book has been to describe the discovery and treatment of karmic injuries and removal of earthbound souls from the aura. How about some positive aura medicine? This would involve avoidance of injury, of course. It seems logical to plan one's next incarnation and avoid ingesting drugs, smoking, or taking part in harmful activities. Meditation and clearing of the energy field could become as routine as brushing one's teeth. In order to be most effective, I try to keep my energy very clean, and I am very rarely troubled by life's little problems. One could be especially careful in checking into hospitals, going to discos, or frequenting bars and smoky places, where addicted earthbound entities might be seeking a free ride. I have discovered how I am able to shield my energy from unwanted influences.

The Future of Aura Surgery

The initial part of aura surgery, resolving release of karmic blockages, has changed very little. My methods of resolving long-standing issues have remained unchanged over the years I have worked in this field.

By the usage of nonlinear systems analysis (NLSA), karmic blockages can be detected both at a glandular level and their impact on the physical organs.

The second part of aura surgery involves surgery on the spiritual internal organs, bones, and joints. This has evolved and will continue to evolve. When I began my aura surgery in 1998, I operated in close proximity to the physical body. Some years later, I discovered that anatomical models can be used as surrogates. This discovery had its origin in that I had only a scant knowledge of human anatomy. I'm not a medical doctor or medical therapist. For this reason, I bought myself an anatomical model of the human body and placed it next to me on a table during the treatment.

When I tested a client's aura and felt a blockage in the body, I could compare it with the model and discover where the problem existed more exactly. It removed a lot of guesswork. After using the model for a few months, I wondered what would happen if the client would hold the model while I touched it and probed various organs for a reaction. Then, something occurred which I hadn't expected, and it was almost impossible to believe. Most clients felt exactly the same pressure in or on their bodies that I was using on the model! So I began to operate on the model and was surprised and pleased to find that aura surgery on the model worked equally well in most instances. Not every client is able to feel the pressure when I use the model. If this is the case, I must operate directly in the aura. I have seen no difference in the results. I believe that the model enhances visualization of a healing as well as locating problems more easily. I am able to focus my energy more exactly on the troubled area.

I was very fortunate at the beginning of my career in aura surgery that I knew physicians in Switzerland, Austria, and Germany that used alternative medicine and were interested in my work. They were more than willing and able to give me guidance. Some of them even allowed me to work in their offices.

Usually the doctors participated in the treatment and their professional knowledge was brought to bear on my psychic abilities and energies. Sometimes I was guided step-by-step by licensed physicians as I performed my spiritual surgery because some of these doctors were actual surgeons! As I write this now, I see some humor in the situation. These were extraordinary people who worked with me, and I am grateful every day for their help. Their steps were being guided as well. I understand that I don't have the scientific knowledge because I base my treatment on pure intuition and guidance.

I was always astounded when doctors confirmed my diagnoses and agreed exactly with my treatment and surgical method. They would even explain why the treatment or surgery was correct. My confidence in my spiritual guides grew every day. My knowledge of anatomy and organic function deepened more and more.

In 2003, one of my physician friends gave me a gift of a wonderful anatomical atlas depicting all the organs, bones, and joints with color illustrations. Soon after, I began to use these images as a surrogate. Often, the client showed no reaction when I used the model but would respond to the pictures. I gradually acquired a large collection of models for all the major organs, joints, and the spine

In 2008, I discovered that is possible to treat clients with acupuncture using images in the anatomical atlas.

I had an interesting experience during a demonstration at a conference in Germany. I asked if someone in the audience was suffering with back pain at that moment. A man raised his hand and came up to the stage. I handed him a picture depicting the muscles of the back and asked him to hold the picture. I then used a needle and touched it to the picture at various points in the lower spine. A video camera and projector enabled the audience to watch the entire procedure. Then the man felt the prick of the needle in his back at exactly the same point I was touching on the photo and reacted to it.

I was facing the audience, and it startled me to see that

several people had obviously also felt the prick! People in the audience were also reacting with excitement. I could see people stirring and commenting; four or five people were talking at once that they felt the prick in their own back muscles at the same time! One person even cried out with an "ouch!" as I pricked the picture. The more the needle was moved on the image, the more people responded and felt the movements. After a short time, they said that they felt warmth on this spot and then the pain disappeared.

This was the first time this happened, but I was soon to learn that it was not the last time. It is now commonplace at demonstrations and it is the Law of Resonance at work wherein energy and information is transmitted. Later, after the demonstration, several of those people came up to me and reported that they had also suffered with back tension for a long time.

This method of aura surgery makes it possible now for many doctors to believe that my methods have value. Doctors now come to me regularly to sit and listen and watch. They ask questions and wonder how they can use some of this knowledge in their own work. Since 2007, I've begun to give seminars to share my accumulated knowledge with doctors and therapists who are interested in learning about aura surgery.

In 2009, I was invited to attend a medical conference at a university in Simferopol, which is located in the Ukraine. I was able to give a presentation on aura surgery with a demonstration at the end.

For doctors and scientists in the former Soviet Union, the idea of aura surgery was nothing new or surprising, as they routinely apply theories of quantum physics in their practice. I was especially astounded that the dean of the medical faculty at this university referred to karma in his presentation! This would be unheard of in any university that I know of in Western Europe—and I suspect in

America also. He spoke of karma as being an influence on health. For me, that showed the beginning of a new orientation and belief system.

Of course, that does not mean that every problem can be treated with aura surgery. It will probably only play a marginal role. Traditional surgery will always be in the first position, especially in regard to acute disease and emergency surgery for accident victims. We are fortunate that medical science has advanced to the level where hands and fingers may be reattached successfully. I have the highest admiration for the wonderful work being done today by our skilled surgeons and scientists.

In case of chronic pain, aura surgery can be a possibility after traditional methods have failed.

For me, aura surgery also has a theological aspect. Many people in these times have little or no relationship with the traditional image of God that is portrayed by major religions. Some believe that there is no God and that creation is a chance result of evolution.

However, when I look at the anatomical illustrations, I realize just how awesome this creation of a human being really is. I marvel at how the individual cells and organs are created and matched and how the intelligence that must be behind it is indescribable. I have only the deepest reverence for this intelligence. It is the spiritual intelligence of which Max Plank spoke, which binds everything in the universe together.

This realization makes me reverent and filled with awe in my daily work. If I want to meet God, I will not find him in books or religious texts. He meets me in every human being and aspect of creation and especially in this person who is facing me at this moment.

—Gerhard

A Word of Caution

It would be very important here to insert a note of caution to individuals who would like to emulate Gerhard and perform apparent miracles of healing with aura surgery. Gerhard is constantly learning from books, doctors, and medical articles about the workings of the human body and effects of illness, injuries, and treatments. This is not to say that his education is equal to a graduate from a medical school, but his unique abilities bring a new set of guidelines and rules to treatment. A perfect physician/healer would understand both fields. Alas, most medical schools do not teach any courses on the human energy field. His strongest desire is to teach medical professionals and therapists about the energy patterns that surround the individual and interpretation of that energy as it relates to treatment of a patient. A person trained in Reiki, for example, with little or no understanding of medicine and anatomy would not be able to react to a client who suddenly loses consciousness because an old injury or wound has been touched. Indeed, trained physicians might also wonder at a sudden, inexplicable physical change in a patient. A dangerous situation might be created and the well-intentioned healer might create an emergency because he has inadvertently touched upon an old wound or crisis.

19

Doris Discovers She Is Also a Medium

I WANT TO INCLUDE my personal experiences in this book about Gerhard. It was because of these experiences that this book came into being. I've been a dabbler in esoteric things my entire life. I've had some experiences that could only be considered paranormal; I've had several out-of-body experiences that were my personal proof that consciousness survives outside the physical body. When I met Gerhard, I was deeply impressed by his sincerity and earnestness. There is nothing in his appearance to indicate that he has unusual psychic abilities—no flowing robe, no Eastern jewelry—but I quickly learned that he is a master at what he does.

I organized a three-day workshop in Amado, Arizona, for Gerhard. We rented a bungalow on the banks of the Santa Cruz River (which is dry most of the year) with a view of the Santa Rita Mountains. The Amado Territory Inn was the setting for this workshop, and the atmosphere was perfect. There were about seventeen participants in all—a very good number.

Gerhard uses music—all kinds of music—to build

energy in a room, and the Amado workshop was no exception. A typical workshop will begin with some lively and energetic rock numbers and gospel tunes. Gerhard encourages the participants to move their hands, move their feet, move their bodies, and dance to the music. He was dancing with us. Most people begin slowly and self-consciously and with a bit of shyness, but the music brings them into motion. Soon, some of them are dancing with abandon, and the more inhibited ones begin to smile and loosen up also.

He began the Amado workshop at nine o'clock on Friday morning with some lively and energetic rock numbers and gospel tunes. People who expect only classical or spiritual selections are surprised and laugh out loud when they hear Wanda Jackson roaring, "Let's have a party!" We did dances from the sixties—jumping around the room and laughing at ourselves and one another. We accepted one another as partners in this energy process. Gerhard believes that rock-and-roll music from the fifties and sixties is enormously liberating.

The dancing, laughing, and sharing of high-energy music united the group in a vital way. After a warm-up period, which lasted about forty-five minutes, the participants were ready to collapse into a chair or onto the floor and get into some serious meditation. Each morning of the seminar began with some kind of activity that seemed to energize the room.

I noticed something peculiar, though, as we were dancing around the room and laughing. I felt something falling into my hair. Some fine substance, like cobwebs, was landing on my face and arms. I brushed it away and noticed one or two others doing the same thing. I could see nothing unusual, and I didn't understand it at all. I thought we had knocked some cobwebs loose from the ceiling, but this beautiful house was too new for cobwebs. I remarked on this to Gerhard, and he smiled. He said he thought it was what the spiritualists call ectoplasm. Wow! That meant that the spirits were dancing with us!

When the dancing was over and participants had settled down on chairs, sofas, and the floor, Gerhard announced that he would allow us to come to him and feel his aura. He would then ask for an earthbound entity to come into his aura. He would allow an earthbound spirit to share his energy and space, and then show the group how to feel the energy and release it. This announcement had the impact of a shockwave in the room. Hands shot up all over with questions, questions, questions. Many in the room were frightened or anxious. Some were concerned about the entire idea of what they deemed spirit possession. The movie *The Exorcist* had a large audience and had raised a lot of fear in people's minds. Gerhard pointed out that his so-called possession would be something that he would allow and invite. He also said that the Catholic Church performed exorcism rituals in a confrontational and hostile way. He could and would remove the entity much more effectively in a loving way.

First, he invited each participant to feel his aura! One by one, they lined up and passed by him as he stood quietly in the middle of the room. Classical music played softly in the background, and we felt his aura one at a time. Then, each of us was asked to remember the experience and how his aura felt to us. I was the last to go to Gerhard. My personal experience was that his aura was uniform in feeling and temperature around his body. It seemed to me to be very warm and vibrant. Others reported different feelings and impressions. Some reported feelings of warmth; some felt motion or a heaviness; and a few reported seeing mental pictures. I noticed nothing remarkable.

He then announced that he would ask his guides to send an earthbound entity into his aura. He closed his eyes for about ten seconds and then announced that he had one.

There was utter silence in the room. He then invited us to file by again and see if we could feel any difference in his aura.

Again, I was last, and I was surprised to notice a marked difference. The front of his aura felt exactly the same as it had before. However, in the back, there seemed to be a diffused feeling, as if two energies had been merged. I don't have the words to describe this, but the energy field seemed larger and less organized, for lack of a better word. I felt it as thick as pea soup with slight motion within. I can still recall my impressions of his aura both times.

After everyone had filed past, he showed us how he could remove the earthbound from his personal energy field and send it into the light. He said that he would first ask for understanding and pardon from the entity and explain that he could not share Gerhard's body and that he wasn't in the right place. He mentally explained to the entity that he or she had been forgiven for any errors in this life and that a light could be seen if the entity would only look up, that it was time to move toward the light, and that friends and loved ones were looking down to help guide the way to the light.

Sometimes, it might be necessary to turn the entity's head so that the light could be seen by the entity. It would then slide up and out, presumably passing into the light. His use of the word head made no sense to me at all since my impressions were of a cloud of energy. I'm sure that was a deficiency on my part. Gerhard has a lot more experience with this!

After only a few seconds, Gerhard announced that the entity was gone.

This demonstration was quite provocative and moving. It didn't quite prepare me for my personal experience the following day, however. On Saturday, the second day of the workshop, after the rock music and dancing, Gerhard changed the music to a classical piece. Speaking very softly, he asked us to free our minds and prepare for meditation. As it happened, it was a chakra meditation. I have participated in numerous meditations, and I even studied and practiced past life regressions in the seventies, but never before had I experienced anything like what happened to me next.

Having learned the art of hypnosis in the seventies, I'm notoriously difficult to hypnotize. I don't fully cooperate with a guided meditation, as I'm always critically analyzing the technique and the hypnotist. I don't let myself really go under, even though I know I'm capable of being hypnotized to the deepest levels. For me, it's a matter of trust. With Gerhard, however, there's such a trust that he could never do or think anything harmful or negative, and that he could understand and explain whatever happened. That supreme trust enabled me to slip into a meditative state very easily. Normally, I don't stay at a deep level long enough to really experience anything of a significant or moving nature. But today, the experience would be different.

Gerhard called upon four angels to bring peace, love, wisdom, and harmony to the land. I remember my consciousness soaring above the landscape like an eagle. The music streamed under my feathers as I soared and dived. I was so peaceful that it came as a rude shock when something whacked the back of my canvas chair and hit my back and shoulders so hard that I was propelled forward along with the chair. I opened my eyes and saw that I was the only one so disturbed—and that the culprit who had disturbed me so violently was not in sight. Gerhard's eyes were closed while he was speaking to the group in quiet, level tones.

I was fully awake and fully perplexed! What happened? Earthbound?! I knew it must be an earthbound! I felt very still inside with no emotions or pain, but I did hear one word repeating in my mind: *waiting*. I waited almost without moving with this heavy feeling upon my back and shoulders until Gerhard finished the meditation. I heard the word waiting two or three more times. Apparently, no one else in the room had been so affected, as they were all relaxed and happy. I didn't feel any discomfort or pain, just the heaviness and this waiting attitude.

As soon as Gerhard finished, the others began relating their feelings during the meditation. I sat silently and waited. Gerhard then called for a ten-minute break.

I rose and walked straight to him and asked him to check my aura.

He looked closely at my face, put his hands up, and quietly said, "Yes, you have one."

He then removed it. I felt something filmy slide straight up over my shoulders and head, something like the feeling of removing a silk garment. The weight was no longer there, and I felt normal again.

I asked Gerhard, "What does it mean? I've never had such an experience in my life before."

He replied, "Your guides may have sent him to you to demonstrate the truth of what you are learning."

Well, of course, I always need personal proof, and there it was!

As it turned out, I was to receive more personal proof the following day.

Did I Need More Proof?

The next day, however, provided a different kind of proof. Again, it was during a guided meditation. I was seated in a different director's chair, feeling relaxed and comfortable. This time, something struck my left shoulder, and my neck began to hurt immediately. The impact was lighter than the one I experienced the day before, and I thought at first that it was just a muscle twitch or spasm. The neck pain was something else. I turned my head this way and that and got no relief. And then, a deep sadness just fell over me. Just ten minutes before, I had been happy and pain-free, and now I was sad and had a pain in the neck! I felt it could be another earthbound, but why had my guides sent me something that depressed and hurt me so? Another lesson?

Again, I waited until Gerhard had finished his meditation before I approached him and told him that I thought I had another one. He raised his arms to check my aura, and sure enough, he confirmed my feeling. Gerhard thought this entity had been killed, involved in an accident, or possibly hanged, which would explain the neck pain. In any event, he removed the earthbound, and again, I felt the weight slip away, along with the pain. This time, I was a little unsettled. Enough was enough.

"Gerhard, what do I do if this happens again and you're not here?" I asked.

"I will teach you how to remove them by yourself. If that fails, you can always call me, and I will do it over the telephone."

This gave me some comfort, but not as much as I would have liked.

An Answer to an Old Question

Sunday evening, after the workshop had finished and the participants left for home, Gerhard and I cleaned up, packed up, and drove back to my home in Green Valley, Arizona, where he was staying as our guest. I started thinking very strongly of the event that had broken up my first marriage twenty-three years before. The details of this are relayed in the first chapter. I wondered if I could get some answers to questions that I still had about the death of Martin, a good friend, who had died so tragically.

I asked Gerhard if we could ask his spirit guides for answers to my questions. I recognized that this was an unusual request and that Gerhard was a healer, not a séance medium with messages from the dead. Nevertheless, he readily agreed to try.

When we got home, I went to the garage and found an old file containing some documents and photos from this time period. I brought the file in and laid it on the coffee table. Gerhard was in his room, preparing for our session. I sat on the sofa and opened the file. I began to sort through the papers and picked up a photo of my deceased friend.

As I held the photo in my hand, I felt an inner trembling begin. Then, I felt something just pass into my whole body! Every atom of my body seemed to have a different quality. The feeling was indescribable. At no time in my life had I ever had such a feeling. It was very intense, very personal, and very real. The feeling was somewhat like my consciousness had moved to the left side of my body and something else was quietly occupying the right side.

At that moment, Gerhard came out of his room and stopped short. He looked at me and said simply, "He's here."

I nodded but couldn't speak; I literally felt paralyzed. Gerhard sat down beside me on the sofa.

After a few seconds, he spoke. "Everything's okay now. You are not to worry—it was suicide, not murder. He's all right now. He wants you to know that he's with you a lot."

Gerhard went on to say that no one was at fault for what had happened. An enormous feeling of relief and calm then came over me. I hadn't realized until that moment what a feeling of guilt and hostility I still felt over those long-ago events.

I must note for the reader that I'd never relayed the story of this failed early marriage and the death of my friend to Gerhard. It had long ago been put into storage, and I didn't realize until that moment how important it still was to my unconscious feelings of rejection and betrayal.

For some months after that, I had no more experiences with earthbound entities, although I was a bit uneasy for some time. I felt they would not come into my aura without my permission, but I wasn't willing to give that permission unless Gerhard was nearby to release them. Although he assured me that I could remove any influences myself, I wasn't ready to test it. Later events became more and more dramatic as my guides introduced me to my own personal abilities. I now believe that they will not come into my aura without my permission, and I have had many experiences of clearing them alone.

Upon later analysis, I'm convinced that in all these events, I shared my physical body with another being for a short time. An earthbound entity had been helped, and I had experienced a great truth. I was very happy that I had been given this very personal and subjective demonstration of what Gerhard had been teaching and an additional personal proof of the survival of the human spirit. Sometimes, I wonder about the personality of that earthbound soul, whether it was a male or female, what his or her life had been like, and why it had been unable to leave the earth's vibration without help from Gerhard.

While this was an intense and highly charged experience for me, Gerhard seemed to regard it as commonplace. I later learned that it was indeed an everyday experience for him. He told me that this happened frequently at the workshops. He believes that there is some kind of cosmic bulletin board or information available in the spirit plane where they know where he'll be working. They are seeking opportunities for spiritual growth too!

This newfound sensitivity allowed me to conduct a private "house healing" for a property that I had listed for far too long. It was the scene of a suicide and I had often sensed the presence of the former occupant. It wasn't a bad energy, he was just curious about what was to happen to his home. I'm not a dowser myself, but using Gerhard's techniques, I was able to heal the energy and request that he look for his guides and move to the next phase of his existence. He left easily and peacefully. The house was under contract within 6 weeks.

Mother and Child

These events somewhat prepared me for what would happen at Gerhard's next workshop six months later. I'd had a lot of time to absorb what had happened, and I'd had no further experiences. Gerhard repeated his demonstration of how an earthbound entity could enter his aura and be released. At the end of this demonstration, we had a meditation, and I suddenly felt something pass into my body again. I felt twinned or out of focus somehow, but I was very conscious of who I was and what was happening. I could also speak, and I told Gerhard that I had an entity. He decided to let the other participants feel my aura and release the entity. So they gathered around me in a semicircle.

Gerhard stood off to the side and then asked a question. "Do you feel like it is a male or female?"

Something new happened. I heard a clear, masculine voice in my right ear say, "She died in childbirth."

I repeated the sentence to the ones gathered around me. At that moment, a sharp pain hit my groin area, and I felt slimy inside from head to toe.

As the others lifted the spirit from my aura, I felt what I could only term rapture in my heart. I felt so filled with light and joy that I still cannot express it fully with words. My breast literally filled up with joy and gratitude. I believe I felt exactly what the entity was experiencing, and that heaven was rejoicing at the return of this soul. I felt as if

I'd personally managed a beautiful and great deed. I was grateful to my guides for giving me this experience. What an incredible feeling of peace and sanctity was flooding my body. If this is what it feels like to go home, then I'm looking forward to that ultimate experience!

It was time to break for lunch.

While the others went off to munch sandwiches and fruit, I could think of nothing else but what had just happened to me. I sat down to think about it. As I sat there, I suddenly felt something clutching at my right shoulder. Oh, no! I had the thought that I had a monkey hanging onto my arm and shoulder. A monkey! Or a big bird with claws! No, a monkey! This was something new again—just on my shoulder and right arm. What's going on now?

I went off to find Gerhard to get help for this new problem. I found him in the dining room, and my face must have told a story of its own. He looked at me in a puzzled way and laid down his fork.

Very excited, I asked him to please check my right arm and shoulder.

He did and then smiled at me and said, "Doris, you have a baby."

I was astounded! The poor little one. We must have sent his mother along and left him behind!

Gerhard called the others back to the workshop room so they could feel the baby's aura. I'm not sure they all felt him, but I surely did! He was still clutching me, and I felt his panic and terror. I wanted to console him, and I tried to send loving and reassuring thoughts of safety.

We didn't keep him with us very long but dispatched him to his mother, who must have been overjoyed to have him with her again. He was very, very easy to release. I was then able to eat lunch, but with some very deep thoughts indeed. My guides are certainly giving me some important demonstrations today! What did it all mean?

I'm still not sure what to do with these mediumistic abilities, which I've just recently discovered. I'm not planning to open shop or hold séances, but this ability surfaces now and then—on an as-needed basis, it seems. After these experiences in Gerhard's workshops, I know I'll never be the same again. It's one thing to read metaphysical books for a lifetime and discuss survival of the spirit for years. Until you have a personal experience, it's never exactly real—just a theory or belief system which can be altered with new evidence. This new knowledge was just that—knowledge!

From my childhood, I've had many psychic experiences and uncanny occurrences. I've had out-of-body experiences and precognitive dreams, but never anything like what I experienced at Gerhard's workshops. I'm beginning to have unusual experiences at home during and after meditation. I know my soul is sometimes vibrating at a higher frequency and that I will experience more and more, but I still don't know what I'm supposed to do with this or where it's all going. These are questions for me to ponder.

Many psychics believe that the earth and its inhabitants are experiencing some type of vibratory change and that a new step or change of some kind is about to occur. They claim that this change in frequency will enable more and more people to discover their abilities and true selves in the coming years. Children born now into this vibration may take psychic experiences as a matter of fact—perhaps even normal! I wonder what will happen to those who do not experience this new step or change. This planet is surely changing. I believe that it will become clearer as time goes by and that my guides will lead me. I know that understanding will come at the right time.

20

Back in Tucson, Arizona

April 2011

HE'S BACK IN TUCSON, Arizona, after nine years. It's been very busy for him in Europe, and his reputation is now firmly established in the healing circles of European capitals. His energy has changed—radically. He's grown in strength and confidence. He's realized some truths, and he's found some new questions. He's no longer shocked or amazed at the events unfolding in his life. He's become accustomed to daily miracles, which seemed to be interesting coincidences in the past.

I spotted him immediately in the group, standing around the carousel, waiting for the baggage to come down. He looked the same, but as he spotted me and started toward me, I felt the difference immediately. Instead of the usual embrace and kiss on the cheek, I was wrapped in his arms, and I closed my eyes. His energy had changed. I was struck by how powerful it had become.

As we waited outside the terminal for our car to arrive, he spoke excitedly about being in Tucson again, where the night air feels so warm and sweet, especially at this time of year. A full moon was already high in the night sky, and Gerhard was so pleased to be back. He feels at home here in Arizona; he could make a home here for himself quite easily. He loves the air and the mountains and the rocks and trees and the cactus and the flowers. Everyone who has chosen to live here understands that romance.

On the way to the restaurant, he spoke of some of his experiences in the last year as things began to move more quickly for him, as events kaleidoscoped together. His life has unfolded in ways that he could never have foreseen, but always in a straight line, always as if in a plan. He knows there's a plan and we are moving inexorably toward an outcome that is desired by a higher power (or our higher selves?). It's more than we can conceive with our conscious brains. We only receive glimpses of this power, this plan, but I sometimes feel as if we are pawns in some great game and that it is totally unimportant whether we understand the strategy or the outcome at this point. It is important to keep moving forward in our pursuit of understanding.

In the restaurant, he spoke of an interesting fact (I can't say coincidence anymore). On his first trip to Arizona, we had met Dorothy Summers and Alyce Revella, pastors at the Church of Tamara in Tucson. They were the first ones to extend a welcome to him in Tucson and invite him to speak to their group. It was a Friday evening, and as he mounted the podium, I slid over beside Dorothy in the back row and listened to Gerhard speak. At one point, I leaned over and whispered, "What do you think about him?"

She'd responded simply, "Honey, he's a master."

She was so impressed with his abilities that she telephoned a friend in Toronto, Ontario, who was suffering from an inoperable brain tumor. Her friend drove down to Tucson immediately to meet Gerhard. That's a very long trip. She asked for and received an appointment with him. Upon her return to Toronto, she visited her doctor, who examined her and could find no trace of the tumor. It had vanished.

At the time, we considered that to be only one of the

many healings which Gerhard had brought about. As it turned out, it was one of the more significant healings of his career.

In 2003, Gerhard met Clemens Kuby, a prize-winning documentary filmmaker, and his wife, Astrid. Kuby was planning a documentary film on energy healing and asked Gerhard to participate in the film. He was very impressed with Gerhard's work and mentioned his name to a physician associate in Berlin in 2005. The doctor immediately recognized Gerhard's name. She had heard of him before. She had an acquaintance in Toronto, another physician, who had told her about the healing of the brain tumor. The story of the vanishing tumor had traveled from Tucson to Toronto to Berlin to the ears of the German doctor who had already heard of Gerhard when Clemens Kuby mentioned the name again!

There was an unbroken thread from Tucson to Toronto to Berlin!

Epilogue

DO YOU KNOW THE Moon?

Yes, it comes out at night and is three hundred thousand kilometers away from the Earth.

Do you know the Sun?

Yes, it rises in the East, sets in the West, and is millions of miles away from the Earth.

Do you know the World?

Yes, it has seven continents and revolves around the Sun.

Do you know Love?

Yes, there are thousands of books and films about Love, and I've seen many of them.

You really know nothing of all these things!

You don't know the light of the Moon that, silvery in the night, bewitches the World, leaving you with a trace of homesickness and showing you the eternal motion of its coming and going.

Because, even without knowing this, you can still exist.

You don't know the warming energy of the Sun that penetrates deep in your heart and connects you to the Fountain of Life, with which you can see Nature's palette of colors.

Because, even without knowing this, you can still exist.

You don't know the variety of the World, its mountains, valleys, lakes, and oceans that nourish you and give you the earth under your feet.

Because, even without knowing this, you can still exist.

You don't know the feeling of Love, that feeling of being connected to everything that exists and that feeling of a union with the Sun and Moon in your Heart.

Because, even without knowing this, you can still exist.

But you will never really live. Your life will be as an empty calendar page, on which time moves without leaving a trace, like a book without words. Only when Love writes on the pages with the language of Life, then Knowing shall give you the wisdom of Eternal Life. If you have Love in you, further seeking is at an end, and you will have Eternal Life.

—Gerhard Klügl, August 2000

Quotes from Albert Schweitzer

UNDER NO CIRCUMSTANCES DO I want to be a run-of-the-mill person.

I have the right to distinguish myself whenever and wherever I can.

I want to have opportunities and not security.

I do not want to be a citizen dependent on social assistance—humiliated and dull because the government supports me.

I want to take risks, have desires and achieve them, suffer defeats and victories.

I refuse to sell my impetus for a pittance.

I prefer to face the difficulties of life to a secure existence. Better the exciting tension of personal success than the dull peace of Utopia.

I shall not sacrifice my freedom for good deeds nor my human dignity for alms.

I have learned to think and act for myself, to look the world straight in the eye and recognize that this is my Achievement

About the Authors

GERHARD KLUEGL, born in
Germany to refugees from
the former Czechoslovakia,
was a successful patent and
trademark researcher by profession. His innate curiosity
led him to research the power
of music, astrology, dowsing,
reincarnation, mediumship,
and healing. He realized he
had a special gift for healing,
and in the development of
these abilities, discovered
that he was also a medium,

connecting people to their past lives in order to explain
problems or illnesses in today's world. Since 1988, he is a
full time aura surgeon and conducts workshops and private
healing sessions with doctors and naturopathic physicians
in Europe. He has seen and helped thousands of people
since that time. He has achieved international recognition,
including the European Healing Prize in 2005, and has been
the subject of several documentaries and films in Europe.

He is much in demand for healings and workshops and has helped thousands of people.

Gerhard lives in Liechteinstein and has an office in Switzerland. His full-time occupation now is conducting workshops and teaching doctors and health professionals his unique techniques of aura healing. He is living proof that alternative healing methods, including aura surgery, past life regressions, and energy healing, can be used for successful treatment of disease and chronic conditions when traditional medicine is unable to help.

Gerhard's first book, *Quantenland* was written in cooperation with Tom Fritze, and published by Arkana Verlag in 2012.

DORIS SCHATZ was born in Kentucky and has lived in Illinois, Texas, Arizona and Germany. She is married to a retired German soldier and they have two grown sons living in Germany. She has worked as a Secretary, Paralegal, Past Life Regression Hypnotist, Musician, English Teacher, Business Manager, and Real Estate Broker.

Now retired and living in Arizona, she researches energy healing, reincarnation, and mediumship. Her other hobbies are music, reading, and genealogy. She is very interested in reincarnation along DNA lines, and would like to see more research in this area. *Down the Ages* is her first book based on her friendship with Gerhard and personal observation of his abilities.

CPSIA information can be obtained
at www.ICGtesting.com
Printed in the USA
FFOW03n1828121113

9 781627 870252